AUSTRALIAN SEASHORES IN COLOUR

Frontispiece: The vermilion biscuit star, *Pentagonaster dubeni*.

AUSTRALIAN SEASHORES in COLOUR

Keith Gillett
John Yaldwyn

CHARLES E. TUTTLE COMPANY
Rutland, Vermont & Tokyo, Japan

The authors dedicate this book to their mentors and colleagues at the Australian Museum, Elizabeth Carrington Pope and the late Frank Alexander McNeill.

This Tuttle edition is the only edition authorized for sale in North America, South America, Middle East, and Asia

Published by the Charles E. Tuttle Company, Inc. of Rutland, Vermont and Tokyo, Japan with editorial offices at Suido 1-chome, 2-6, Bunkyo-ku, Tokyo, Japan by special arrangement with A. H. & A. W. Reed, Wellington, Auckland, and Sydney

© *1969 by Keith Gillett and John Yaldwyn*

All rights reserved

Library of Congress Catalog Card No. 77-109409

Standard Book No. 8048 0861-9

PRINTED IN JAPAN

Introduction

IN 1952, WILLIAM DAKIN produced a book called *Australian Seashores*, which has become for Australia what F. S. Russell and C. M. Yonge's classic *The Seas* and other works by authors such as E. F. Ricketts and J. Calvin, D. P. Wilson and A. C. Harding have become for the northern hemisphere shores of Europe and America. Having known and worked with the two dedicated biologists who assisted Dakin with his splendid book, we have long felt that something more was needed to present to the interested reader the essential dimension of colour so striking on our Australian seashores. Massive use of colour photography was not practicable for Dakin, but now techniques and printing methods can combine to satisfy this need. The present volume then is our attempt to complement Dakin's important book and to provide a varied selection of colour plates of Australian shoreline features and intertidal and shallow-water animals and plants.

The island continent of Australia stretches north and south through 33 degrees of latitude from the tropical, coral-studded waters of Torres Strait to the cool, temperate, kelp-lined shores of southern Tasmania. From west to east the continent spreads through 38 degrees of longitude—from Shark Bay

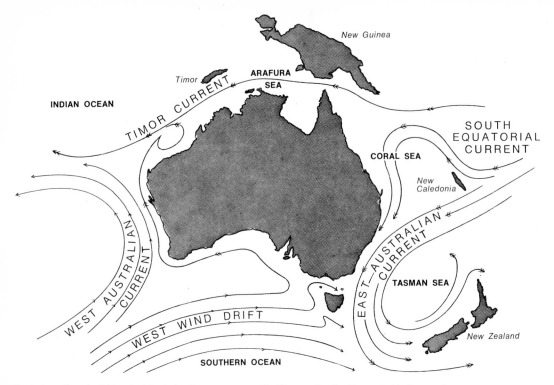

Fig. 1. Australia and neighbouring islands showing warm currents (double arrows) and cold currents (single arrows).

on the shores of the Indian Ocean to Cape Byron at the edge of the Tasman Sea. The Tropic of Capricorn, usually regarded as the southern boundary of the tropical zone, passes right across Australia at the level of the southern end of the Great Barrier Reef (fig. 2). Thus the northern half of the continent is in the tropics while the remainder is geographically in the temperate zone.

To the north of Australia lies the large island of New Guinea and to the north-west lies Timor, the nearest of the multitude of islands forming the Indonesian Archipelago. To the east lies New Caledonia and New Zealand—the former tropical, with its own barrier reef, and the latter, temperate. Beyond the coastline of Australia, as from the coasts of most continents and major islands, there extends a gently sloping, shallow extension of land down to a depth of about 100 fathoms (600 feet). This is called a continental shelf. Beyond the edge of this shelf, the angle of slope of the sea bottom increases greatly as the continental slope passes down into the ocean depths (fig. 4). The continental shelf of

Australia varies greatly in width, extending well beyond the mainland to link Tasmania under Bass Strait in the south, and New Guinea under Torres Strait and the Arafura Sea in the north (fig. 2).

Australia's 12,500 miles of coastline is made up of sandy beaches, rocky cliffs and headlands, tidal mudflats, winding inlets, mangrove swamps and coral reefs in such infinite variety that it is quite impossible to cover this scene and its plant and animal life in one volume of this size. However, a companion book in this series, *The Australian Great Barrier Reef in Colour* by Keith Gillett, covers many aspects of our tropical seashores, so this volume will concentrate mainly on temperate shores but will by no means restrict itself to the southern part of the continent.

For further general reading on the animals and plants of Australia's coasts the four most important books are those by W. J. Dakin, *Australian Seashores*, Angus and Robertson, revised edition 1966; W. Saville-Kent, *The Great Barrier Reef of Australia*, W. H. Allen, 1893; K. Gillett and F. McNeill, *The Great Barrier Reef and Adjacent Isles*, Coral Press, third edition 1967; and Isobel Bennett, *The Fringe of the Sea*, Rigby, 1966.

Recommended, non-specialist yet authoritative books on special groups of Australian seashore plants and animals include the following: A. H. S. Lucas, *The Seaweeds of South Australia*, Government Printer, Adelaide, part I 1936, part II (with Florence Perrin) 1947; H. M. Hale, *The Crustaceans of South Australia*, Government Printer, Adelaide, part I 1927, part II 1929; Joyce Allan, *Australian Shells*, Angus and Robertson, revised edition 1959; O. H. Rippingale and D. F. McMichael, *Queensland and Great Barrier Reef Shells*, Jacaranda Press, 1961; J. Hope Macpherson and C. J. Gabriel, *Marine Molluscs of Victoria*, Melbourne University Press, 1962; H. L. Clark, *The Echinoderm Fauna of Australia*, Carnegie Institute of Washington, 1946; T. D. Scott, *The Marine and Fresh Water Fishes of South Australia*, Government Printer, Adelaide, 1962; T. C. Marshall, *Fishes of the Great Barrier Reef*, Angus and Robertson, 1964; H. Cogger, *Australian Reptiles in Colour*, A. H. & A. W. Reed, 1967; N. W. Cayley, *What Bird is that?* Angus and Robertson, third edition 1959, and E. Troughton, *Furred Animals of Australia*, Angus and Robertson, 9th ed. 1968.

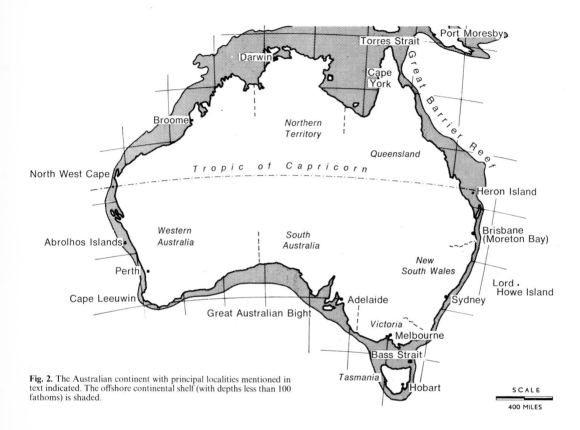

Fig. 2. The Australian continent with principal localities mentioned in text indicated. The offshore continental shelf (with depths less than 100 fathoms) is shaded.

SCALE

400 MILES

Acknowledgements

We wish to thank the following for help during the preparation of this book; Brian Bertram for the skill and patient care applied to the line drawings; T. Barlow, N. Coleman, W. Deas, A. Healy, and C. J. Lawler (collection and photography of marine animals); Miss Elizabeth Pope and the late Frank McNeill; Miss Valerie Jones (algae); W. S. Bertaud and Dr Vivienne Cassie (diatom electron micrographs); Dr C. E. Cutress (sea anemones); Dr D. F. Squires (corals); Dr and Mrs A. H. Banner (snapping shrimp); Dr D. J. G. Griffin (crabs); Dr D. F. McMichael and Jay Richardson (molluscs); Dr N. A. Powell (bryozoans); Dr D. L. Pawson (sea cucumbers); G. P. Whitley (fish); H. G. Cogger (sea snakes); Dr W. H. Dawbin (dolphins) and B. J. Marlow (mammals). Our special thanks go to Miss Ailsa Marshall and to Barbara Yaldwyn for their unfailing encouragement and help during the entire production of this work.

contents

COOL WATERS AND WARM
biogeography

TWO MAIN OCEAN CURRENT SYSTEMS wash around Australia's shores and to a large extent control the temperature of its coastal waters (fig. 1). The warm, westerly-flowing South Equatorial Current approaches eastern Australia from the tropical Pacific Ocean and the main body of this water is deflected southwards down the Queensland and New South Wales coasts as the East Australian Current. The latter brings warm water and many tropical marine plants and animals, (free-swimming or floating at some time during their life history) well down the eastern Australian coastline and has a great influence on the water temperatures of New Zealand as it sweeps back anticlockwise across the southern Tasman Sea. Another branch of the South Equatorial passes through Torres Strait between New Guinea and northern Australia into the Arafura Sea. It then flows along the north-western Australian coastline as the Timor Current and streams on into the Indian Ocean. The cold, easterly-flowing West Wind Drift sweeps through the Southern Ocean south of Australia, and directly influences the water temperatures of Victoria, Tasmania and, to a lesser extent, that of South Australia. A branch of this southern Drift moves up the Western Australian coastline as the West Australian Current and swings anticlockwise out into the Indian Ocean. Inshore from it another branch of the West Wind Drift passes from the Great Australian Bight northwards, as a relatively warm current, to meet the Timor Current off the north-western coastline.

Various names are applied to the different levels and belts of the seashore, including the intertidal zone and sublittoral waters, in different parts of the world. Ones used in this book are shown diagrammatically in fig. 4. In particular the term intertidal is used here for the entire area between the upper limit reached by wind-driven spray at extreme high tide and the lower limit uncovered at extreme low of the lowest spring tide.

Sea surface temperatures around Australia's shores range from a winter minimum of about 8 degrees Centigrade off southern Tasmania to a summer maximum of 32 degrees C and more in the Gulf of Carpentaria, northern Queensland. A study of the distribution of plants and animals around the continent has shown that the coastline can be conveniently classified into three main temperature regions. The extent and overlap of these divisions, called here biogeographic regions, is shown in fig. 5. The tropical region extends from south of the

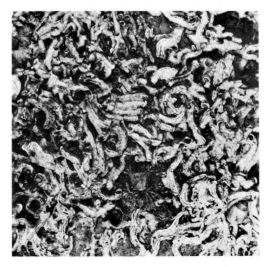

Fig. 3. Intertidal calcareous tubes of the polychaete worm, *Galeolaria caespitosa.*

Plate 3. Cool temperate shoreline with giant bull-kelp, *Durvillea potatorum*, low tide.

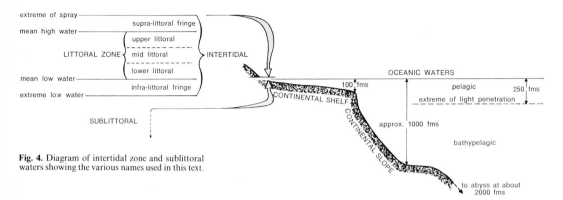

Fig. 4. Diagram of intertidal zone and sublittoral waters showing the various names used in this text.

Abrolhos Islands (fig. 2) in Western Australia, around northern and north-eastern Australia to central New South Wales. The warm temperate region is in two parts: first, a western warm temperate subregion overlapping the southern end of the tropical region in Western Australia and extending around south-western Australia and the Great Australian Bight to the shores of Victoria and southern New South Wales, and secondly, an eastern warm temperate subregion extending from southern Queensland, along the coast of New South Wales to eastern Victoria and north-eastern Tasmania. The overlapping cool temperate region extends from the coasts of Tasmania and Victoria westwards through the Great Australian Bight.

These biogeographic regions, or provinces as they are sometimes called, are thus based on the presence and distributional range of a series of wide-ranging plants and animals selected for various reasons as indicator species. Because the presence or absence of intertidal and shallow water plants and animals is largely controlled by the range of sea temperatures in any one area, species may have a discontinuous distribution near the extremes of their geographic range, depending on their requirements for shelter from exposure to either high or low water temperatures. There are no sharp boundaries around Australia to these biogeographic regions, but rather a gradual change from one to the other with a wide or narrow overlap at each end of a region, depending to some extent on the north-south or east-west trend of the coastline.

In general it is not difficult to recognize the three main regions outlined here. The best indicators are in the zone uncovered, or almost uncovered, at low tide on a reasonably exposed rocky shore. In the cool temperate region the giant bull-kelp *Durvillea potatorum* is typical of this zone (plates 3 & 11) and, in some southern areas, it forms a thick forest of fronds exposed at the surface immediately offshore. In the warm temperate region (typically the eastern warm temperate subregion) cunjevoi, the large sea-squirt *Pyura stolonifera*, characteristically covers the rock in this zone as shown in plate 4. In the tropical region growths of true, stony corals are typical of this same low tidal zone (see plate 5) and by reef formation can modify and extend the actual shoreline itself. A minimum

Plate 4. Warm temperate shoreline with cunjevoi, *Pyura stolonifera*, low tide. ⇨

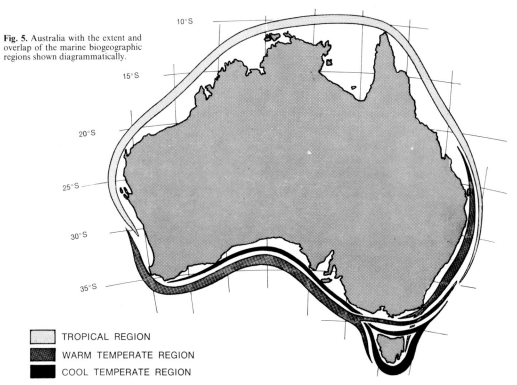

Fig. 5. Australia with the extent and overlap of the marine biogeographic regions shown diagrammatically.

10°S

15°S

20°S

25°S

30°S

35°S

TROPICAL REGION

WARM TEMPERATE REGION

COOL TEMPERATE REGION

winter sea surface temperature of about 20 degrees C corresponds with the southern limits of the tropical region and one of about 13 degrees C with the southern limits of the warm temperate.

Among the intertidal animals and plants, many tend to occur at very definite and often clearly-marked levels on the seashore, and this is especially obvious on steep or moderately-sloping rocky shores (plate 6). This type of natural banding is referred to as intertidal zonation and reflects the interaction of a whole series of factors, such as dessication, exposure to air, exposure to wave action, interrelations between different species, and the actual slope of the rocky shore platform. Thus intertidal plants and animals tend to live at a level matching their degree of adaptation to these factors and matching their ability to obtain sufficient food at whatever tide level is appropriate for them.

On all seashores, the pattern of zoning varies according to the degree of exposure to wave action and direct surf. In sheltered south-eastern Australian waters, a band of the Sydney rock-oyster *Crassostrea commercialis* may cover the shoreline to the virtual

Plate 5. Tropical shoreline with stony corals partly uncovered, low tide.

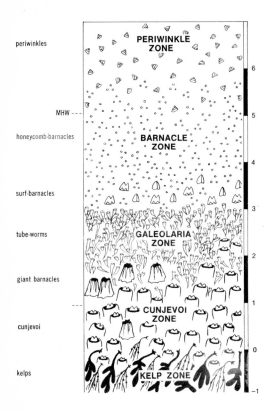

periwinkles

MHW ---

honeycomb-barnacles

surf-barnacles

tube-worms

giant barnacles

cunjevoi

kelps

PERIWINKLE ZONE

BARNACLE ZONE

GALEOLARIA ZONE

CUNJEVOI ZONE

KELP ZONE

6

5

4

3

2

1

0

−1

Fig. 6. Generalised intertidal zonation in eastern warm temperate region under reasonably sheltered conditions.

and below zero on the Sydney tide gauge. In the supra-littoral fringe one finds the littorinid periwinkles *Melaraphɑ unifasciata* (bluish-purple and smooth-shelled) and *Nodilittorina pyramidalis* (plate 37q), often in large numbers and commonly the sole occupants of that level. In the upper half of the littoral a barnacle zone occurs consisting mainly of small, closely-packed honeycomb-barnacles, *Chamaesipho columna*, but with two other surf-barnacles, *Tetraclita rosea* and *Catophragmus polymerus* (fig. 38) usually present towards its lower edge. *Chamaesipho* may completely cover the surface of the rock in some areas (up to 12,500 individuals to the square foot) and thus form a white intertidal band, clearly visible even at a distance. In the lower half of the littoral there is a characteristic zone of encrusting, white, calcareous tubes (fig. 3) secreted by the polychaete worm *Galeolaria caespitosa*. Where these worm-tubes form a massive encrustation, the growth is sometimes inappropriately referred to as "Sydney coral". In the lower part of this *Galeolaria* zone there are often scattered giant barnacles, *Balanus nigrescens*, reaching an individual height of up to 2½ inches. Below the *Galeolaria*, and extending into the infra-littoral fringe, is the cunjevoi zone already referred to as characteristic of the eastern warm temperate subregion (see plate 4). Overlapping and extending below the cunjevoi again is a band characterized by two brown kelps, the laminarian *Ecklonia radiata* (plate 11) and the bubble-weed *Phyllospora comosa* (plate 11).

exclusion of all other animals, but on exposed, surf-beaten rocks the oyster band is replaced by bands of acorn barnacles and limy worm-tubes. Figure 6 is a diagram showing a generalised, intertidal, eastern warm temperate zonation pattern in reasonably sheltered conditions but facing the open ocean. The scale on the right is marked in feet above

Key to opposite page:

Plate 6. Intertidal zonation on rocky shores; metamorphic rocks at Bermagui, NSW (*above*), and granitic rocks at South West Rocks, NSW (*below*).

ROCKS, SAND AND MANGROVES
the intertidal scene

TEMPERATE AUSTRALIAN SEASHORES are either rocky, sandy, muddy, or perhaps a combination of all three. Rocky shores have been dealt with in some detail in the previous chapter and will not be discussed further here. Contrasting examples, such as smooth granitic turtle-backs at South West Rocks, northern New South Wales, steep sediment-ary sandstone cliffs south of Sydney, central NSW, and vertical-sided, surge channels in metamorphic rocks at Bermagui, southern NSW, are illustrated in colour on pages 7 and 17.

Sandy beaches present a very different appearance from such rocky shores. Gone are the attached seaweeds and encrusting animals, for there is no firm surface to which they may attach themselves. In the main sand dwellers are burrowers, spending much of their time beneath the surface, but maintaining direct contact with the surface in one way or another. Characteristic animals of the upper sandy littoral in many parts of Australia are burrowing shore crabs such as the sand-bubbler crab, *Scopimera inflata* (fig. 7), and the largely nocturnal ghost crabs of the genus *Ocypode* (page 9).

The sand-bubbler crab is rarely found on any but open coastal sand beaches where the sea water is clear and free from mud. It commonly occurs in areas where small streams of fresh water cross beaches and its burrows can be found in sand moistened with brackish water seepage. Unlike the allied ghost crabs, *Scopimera* avoids direct exposure to surf and appears to favour flat beaches where waves are usually small and where the rise and fall of the tide leaves the sand relatively undisturbed. In suitable localities large areas of beach sand, hundreds of square yards in extent, may be covered at low tide with countless millions of tiny round sand pellets, left by the feeding activities of a community of these small crabs. Around the mouth of each individual burrow (figs. 7 & 8) these rounded pellets are of a uniform size (pellet size increases with individual crab size) and are roughly arranged in irregular radiating lines

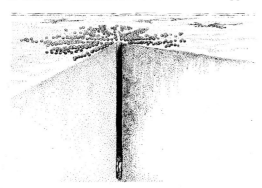

Fig. 7. Cut-away burrow of sand-bubbler crab, *Scopimera inflata*, and surface workings.

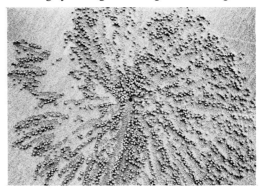

Fig. 8. An individual *Scopimera* burrow-mouth with associated feeding furrows and pellets.

18

Plate 7. Sandspit, Palm Beach, NSW, ocean beach right, estuary left.

from a few inches to about 18 inches in length. Several larger, irregularly-shaped pellets excavated from the burrow itself are scattered among them. As the tide falls the burrow, which may be 15 inches or more deep, is cleared and the large pellets are deposited near the opening. The crab then feeds on the surface of the beach, moving sideways from the burrow and scooping out a narrow furrow with the nippers of the first pair of legs. The surface sand thus scooped up is passed to the mouth-parts, and organic food fragments are sifted out and eaten. The rejected sand grains are manipulated into a rounded pellet, and this pellet is then discarded over the back of the crab as it moves one pace further from its burrow. As the furrows are more or less straight, the pellets are consequently arranged in irregular rows beside them (fig. 8). The sand-bubbler crab, when feeding rapidly, can produce pellets at a rate of about one every 15 seconds, but on the least disturbance it returns directly to its burrow. Upon starting to feed again the crab begins a furrow in a new, apparently random, direction.

Typical sandy beach dwellers of the lower littoral include burrowing bivalve molluscs such as the pipi, *Plebidonax deltoides* (pl. 40m), and the finger-nail shell, *Neosolen correctus* (pl. 40c), to give two examples with very different shapes; carnivorous snails such as the red-mouthed sand snail, *Conuber melastoma* (pl. 38o), adapted for ploughing through the surface of the beach on its greatly expanded foot, and several polychaete worms with well-developed digging organs such as the giant beach-worm, *Onuphis teres* (pl. 26 and fig. 31), which can range up to 8 feet in length. All these animals may have to contend with being smothered by sand and thus having their supply of oxygen reduced. Burrowers in sands and muds, to ensure an adequate supply of dissolved oxygen from fresh seawater,

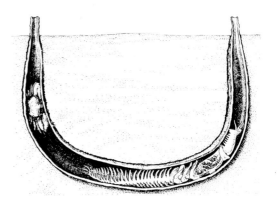

Fig. 9. Parchment-tube worm, *Chaetopterus variopedatus*, with commensal half crab, *Polyonyx transversus*.

are usually equipped with long breathing tubes or siphons which reach up to the surface of their surroundings, or with especially efficient breathing gills, or other aids to respiratory exchange such as special blood pigments. Sand grains and sediments are excluded from gills, siphons and breathing tubes by fringes of hairs or sieve-like papillae.

Between 3,000 and 4,000 years ago, well after the world-wide, major fluctuations of sea-level associated with the Ice Ages of the Pleistocene (largely responsible for the drowned valley and cliff scenery of the central New South Wales coast), a relatively slight drop in temperature caused an increase in land-ice, and a lowering of the world sea-level by 10 to 15 feet. This recent drop exposed sand-bars which, supplemented by wind-blown sands, cut off coastal lagoons and linked rocky coastal islands to the mainland along many parts of the Australian coastline. Plate 7 shows an example of this island-linking where the sandspit beneath the suburb of Palm Beach, north of Sydney, links the rocky island of Barrenjoey to the tip of the Newport-Avalon peninsula. On the right of the spit is a sandy surf

Plate 8. Digging parchment-tube worm, *Chaetopterus variopedatus*, from *Zostera* flats.

beach facing the open sea, a typical habitat of ghost crabs, while on the left is the corner of a sandy mudflat facing Pittwater, an inlet of the Hawkesbury estuary, and a typical habitat of the soldier crab, *Mictyris longicarpus* (page 5 and pl. 35).

Estuarine mudflats form in sheltered inlets where the ebb and flow of tidal waters make the only noticeable current. Drainage from the surrounding land must be small, except after very heavy rain, so that the area becomes a settling place for fine mud which would otherwise be washed out to sea. At low tide sandy mudflats with widths of up to hundreds of yards can be exposed in suitable localities; it is in these eel-grass (*Zostera capricorni*, pl. 8 and fig. 11) covered flats that the parchment-tube worm, *Chaetopterus variopedatus* (fig. 9 and pl. 29), occurs. This extraordinary polychaete worm lives, as its common name implies, in a soft, parchment-like, U-shaped tube, with both ends narrowed and projecting out of the sandy mud like a pair of inch-long drinking straws. *Chaetopterus variopedatus* is notable for four main reasons: its wide distribution outside Australia (it is found in

Fig. 10. Semaphore crab, *Heloecius cordiformis*, at mouth of burrow in mangrove swamp.

North America, Europe, Asia and elsewhere); its complex and fantastic shape (illustrated and discussed on page 62); the commensal (literally "eating together at the same table") relationship between it and a half-crab, *Polyonyx transversus*, which lives with the worm in its tube (this "innkeeping", as it is called, is shown in fig. 9), and its unexpected power of luminescence, or light production (illustrated in pl. 29).

In many estuaries and inlets, especially in tropical and warm temperate regions, tidal mudflats often support a thick growth of mangrove trees. About twenty species of mangroves are found in Australia, but only two reach south to Sydney on the east coast, and only one, the grey or tree mangrove, *Avicennia marina* (pl. 9), extends right around southern Australia to encircle the whole continent. *Avicennia* and some other mangroves have numerous short, vertical root-branches, or pneumatophores, rising closely-spaced from the mud surrounding each tree. It is these pencil-like pneumatophores, with their clusters of attached rock-oysters, and the innumerable crabs and crab-holes, which are so characteristic of Australian mangrove swamps. Fiddler crabs of the genus *Uca*, the semaphore crab *Heloecius cordiformis* (fig. 10), and species of marsh crabs *(Sesarma)* are abundant burrowers in mangrove muds or open flats and salt marshes. Ritual display by males of both *Uca* and *Heloecius*, in which one enlarged nipper, or both equal nippers in *Heloecius*, are waved, jerked or fiddled, has led to the common names applied to these crabs. Mudskippers, fishes which live mostly out of water and climb among the mangrove roots and branches, can be abundant on tropical Australian coasts, and one species, *Periophthalmodon australia*, is shown resting on a mangrove branch in fig. 62.

Plate 9. Temperate grey mangrove, *Avicennia marina*, swamp with pneumatophores.

PLANTS IN THE SEA
algae and eel-grass

THREE MAIN TYPES OF PLANT LIFE are found in the sea. There are microscopic, single-celled, specialised algae called diatoms with tiny, siliceous, external shells formed of two lid-like structures that fit one into the other and enclose the body of the plant in a little capsule. Diatoms, illustrated and discussed in the next chapter, are planktonic; that is, they drift freely in the sea, and their countless numbers are of primary importance in the economy of all marine life. Then there are true algae, or seaweeds proper, to which the great majority of marine, multi-cellular plants belong. Algae are of simpler structure than typical flowering plants of the land and, like the ferns, they reproduce themselves by spores instead of by seeds produced from flowers. Finally there are a very few, true flowering plants such as eel-grasses and their allies.

Algal seaweeds have no true roots and absorb essential minerals as well as oxygen and carbon dioxide directly from sea water. All seaweeds, large and small, contain chlorophyll and, using this unique green pigment, they manufacture food from inorganic materials in the presence of sunlight. Chlorophyll breaks down carbon dioxide present in sea water, setting free a large part of the oxygen and retaining the carbon for use by the plant. The excess oxygen passes back into the water and is thus available for marine animal respiration. Just as in the terrestrial plant-animal relationship, so it is in the sea: all marine animal life depends upon, and has its basis in, the marine plants. A food-cycle links true algae and planktonic diatoms, utilizing light energy from the sun, with invertebrate and fish herbivores; then through intermediate steps, or directly, with carnivores of all sizes, and finally, with oceanic fish and whales. Surface animals, large or small, ultimately provide after death the organic food material for life in abyssal depths.

There are between 1,500 and 2,000 species of algae known from Australia. These are classified on the pigments present and on fundamental differences in structure and life history into three main groups: the greens, the browns (including olive-greens), and the reds. Green algae generally frequent the higher intertidal zones, brown algae are often well-developed in the lower intertidal and subtidal zones, while the reds usually characterise permanently submerged levels. The largest seaweed in Australian waters is a brown kelp, *Macrocystis pyrifera*, occurring along the southern coastline and around Tasmania. It has been recorded locally with fronds up to at least 90 feet in length, but in Patagonian waters the same species may grow to 600 feet in length and is thus the largest plant known.

Fig. 11. Northern eel-grass, *Zostera capricorni*, on estuarine mudflat with mangrove pneumatophores.

Plate 10. The alga, *Caulerpa flagelliformis*, in an intertidal rock pool.

Fig. 12. An agar-producing alga, *Gracilaria secundata*, from south-eastern Australia.

Green algae include the sea-lettuce *Ulva lactuca* (the bright green fronds in pl. 14), which grows seasonally both on exposed rock platforms and in muddy estuaries, as well as the striking *Caulerpa flagelliformis* (pl. 10), a large, flat-fronded alga growing abundantly in some intertidal areas of central New South Wales.

Brown seaweeds already mentioned include *Durvillea*, *Ecklonia* and *Phyllospora* (pls. 3 & 11), all being large kelps of the infra-littoral fringe and below. Another prominent form is Neptune's necklace, *Hormosira banksii* (pl. 18), which often covers considerable areas of the mid-tidal.

Most of the red algae are small plants, but they may be conspicuous because of their colour and form. *Champia compressa* (pl. 11) is brilliantly iridescent, with vivid blue and green colouring when seen in lower intertidal pools, but appears translucent red when taken from the water. *Gracilaria secundata* (fig. 12), from low tide levels in south-eastern Australia, has a rubber-like feel and belongs to a group of agar-producing seaweeds. Coralline algae are either plant-like reds with branching, often jointed, calcareous fronds (*Corallina*, pl. 21), or they form a solid pink encrustation over rocks at the lowest tidal levels (pl. 6 upper). The common calcareous, encrusting forms of south-eastern Australia are usually species of *Lithophyllum*.

Only a few true flowering plants occur in Australian waters and the sea-grasses *Zostera* and *Posidonia* are by far the most abundant. These higher plants have true roots and flowers, and can live completely submerged; they are regarded as having invaded the sea from the land and freshwaters. The algae, in contrast, are presumed to have originated in the sea. *Zostera capricorni*, the northern eel-grass (fig. 11 and pl. 8), is especially abundant on sandy or muddy estuarine shores; other species are found in southern waters. These *Zostera* flats are characteristically rich in decaying vegetable matter derived from eel-grass, and in burrowing worms and crustaceans feeding on this organic food. *Posidonia australis* has a wider and longer leaf-blade than *Zostera* (a single leaf of *Posidonia* can be seen in the right foreground of fig. 11) and grows at a somewhat deeper level. Leaf fibres of *Posidonia* have a high breaking strain and some attempt has been made to exploit this sea-grass commercially in South Australia. Natural balls of these fibres, rolled by wave action, are often washed ashore on southern beaches.

Key to opposite page:

Plate 11. (*Top left*): bubble-weed, *Phyllospora comosa*. (*Top right*): iridescent red alga, *Champia compressa*. (*Bottom left*): the laminarian kelp, *Ecklonia radiata*. (*Bottom right*): holdfasts of giant bull-kelp, *Durvillea potatorum*.

LIVING FLOATERS
plankton

ALL LIVING CREATURES, both animals and plants, which float or drift with the tides and currents are called plankton. This comes from a Greek word meaning "that which is made to wander or drift", in other words drifting beyond its own control. It is useful to have this one word to distinguish all passively-drifting life from free-swimming creatures such as fish and whales which can move at will through the water; these in contrast are called nekton.

Many planktonic creatures are invisible, or only just visible, to the naked eye, but some such as jellyfish may reach several feet across. Many are single-celled, such as diatoms and foraminiferans (fig. 15), but others are highly complex, such as crustaceans (pl. 13) and fish larvae. Many spend the whole of their life history as plankton, but others such as the eggs or young stages of many attached or crawling shore animals (barnacles, shellfish, crabs among others) spend only part. The brief floating existence of such examples favours the spread of crowded populations.

The main differences between animals and plants are in their food and in their manner of feeding.

Fig. 13. The diatom *Biddulphia mobiliensis;* two linked cells, approx. x150 *(left)* and electron micrograph of one shell valve, approx. x850 *(right).*

Fig. 14. Electron micrograph showing detailed structure of siliceous valve wall of *Biddulphia mobiliensis*, (x20,000).

Plate 12. Tropical algal bloom; *Trichodesmium hildebrandtii* from 1,100 ft. *(left)*, and under microscope. approx. x55 *(right).*

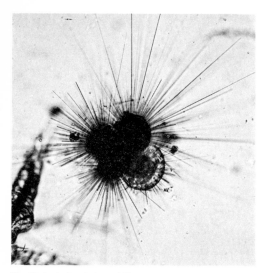

Fig. 15. A planktonic foraminiferan, *Globigerina* species.

The chlorophyll cycle begins in the sea. The upper sunlit layers, rich in dissolved gasses and mineral compounds, provide ideal conditions for plant growth. In these layers microscopic plant life is scattered through the water like a fine aquatic dust, with the organisms floating because of their lightness, though often projections like those of thistledown assist in their suspension. It has been estimated that under average conditions a cubic foot of surface seawater contains about 20,000 diatom-sized plants and at least 12 million smaller plant forms grouped under the general name of flagellates. Comparative figures for planktonic animals, or zooplankton, would be about 120 per cubic foot.

As mentioned in the previous chapter, some diatoms are box-like in form, but many others show a whole range of unusual shapes (fig. 13, for example), even linking together in extended chains of similar individuals. Their external, glass-like shell is not formed of simple sheets of plain silica. The surfaces are in fact microscopically sculptured with all manner of striations, pits and perforations forming a regular, intricate pattern unique to each species. Details of the full complexity and structure of this system of perforations, and the secondary system of perforations from which it is built up, are so fine that they can be revealed only by the electron microscope. Figure 14 is a micrograph of portion of the shell wall of *Biddulphia mobiliensis* enlarged about 20,000 times. This shows clearly the two-layered wall and the double system of perforations penetrating it.

Under certain conditions sudden blooms of diatoms or other single-celled plants, such as blue-green algae or flagellates, can take place, often colouring the surface of the sea over quite large areas. A tropical bloom of the blue-green alga, *Trichodesmium hildebrandtii*, is shown in plate 12. Locally called "coral spawn", such blooms are often seen in Barrier Reef waters in the months of September and October.

Plate 13 gives a good idea of tropical zooplankton with its abundance of varied organisms, including a segmented larval polychaete worm, several copepod crustaceans (lower right; T-shaped, with antennae at right angles to body) and three red-spotted crab larvae, or zoeas (upper right, centre and lower left; with forked tails and prominent dorsal spines). Other planktonic animals illustrated elsewhere include the Portuguese man-of-war and by-the-wind sailor (pls. 15 & 17), various jellyfish (pls. 18 & 19), goose barnacles and their acquired float (pl. 31), the gastropod mollusc, *Recluzia*, and its self-produced float (pl. 36), as well as the giant, colonial sea-squirt, *Pyrosoma* (fig. 61).

Plate 13. Tropical plankton with copepods, polychaete, and crab larvae, x45.

PERFORATIONS AND SPICULES
sponges

THE SIMPLEST OF ALL the multicellular animals of the seashore are the sponges. The irregular growth of many forms does not allow recognition of individual animals and most must be regarded as colonies of numerous individuals growing together. When a sponge colony is broken up, the small pieces can develop into new colonies, provided each piece is large enough to lead an independent existence.

Sponges are sessile animals; they are often encrusting growths and thus irregular in shape, but some from subtidal waters grow in regular and characteristic fan-like, or vase-like forms. Colours are varied, but usually constant for each species.

Within the body of a sponge there is a single, though often complexly-developed cavity. Water passes into this cavity through numerous small pores in the body wall, and is expelled through one or more large openings. Circulation of water is brought about by the beating of countless flagellated cells lining the body cavity. Thus the living sponge is like an animated filter, straining out minute organisms from the water passing through the body.

Sponge tissue is supported by an internal skeleton consisting of a mass of either calcareous or siliceous spicules, or of a network of horny elastic material called spongin. Commercial sponges possess a skeleton of spongin fibres only and are not harvested in Australian waters.

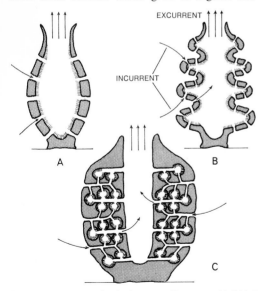

Fig. 16. Sponge types: A, simple sponge; B, sponge with folded body wall; C, complex sponge with system of flagellated chambers. Arrows indicate water movement.

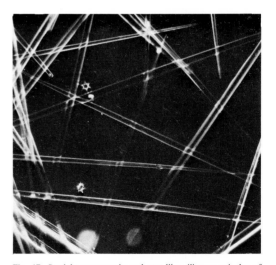

Fig. 17. Straight monaxonic and star-like siliceous spicules of *Tethya corticata* (x100).

Plate 14. The orange sponge, *Tethya corticata,* extreme low tide.

COLONIES THAT SAIL
pelagic coelenterates

THE PORTUGUESE MAN-OF-WAR, or bluebottle (pl. 15), is a well-known member of a large group of almost exclusively marine animals called the Coelenterata, literally the "hollow-gut" animals. In the individual coelenterate the main cavity of the body is the digestive cavity and the mouth is the only opening to the outside. Coelenterates exist in a great variety of shapes and forms and, like sponges, many must be considered as colonies of a number of individuals living together.

There are two basic coelenterate life forms: the polyp and the medusa. The polyp (freely translated, "many feet") is a tubular coelenterate attached firmly or loosely, at one end of the body, to some object or surface and bearing a ring of tentacles around a terminal mouth at the other end. Sea anemones, corals, and the delicate plant-like growths called hydroids are polyps in form, the former invariably solitary and the latter two most commonly colonial. The medusa (named from its resemblance to the head and serpent-hair of the Gorgon Medusa) is a bell-shaped, or inverted saucer-shaped, free-swimming coelenterate. It typically bears a circle of tentacles hanging down from the margin of the bell and the mouth is situated in the middle of the lower surface, often at the end of a tube or some other structure. Jellyfish, both large and small, are medusoid in form and invariably solitary. Both the polyp and medusoid forms alternate in the life cycle of many coelenterates.

A unique feature of the coelenterates as a group is the possession of specialised, microscopic stinging or thread capsules called nematocysts. These occur in great numbers, and in a variety of shapes and

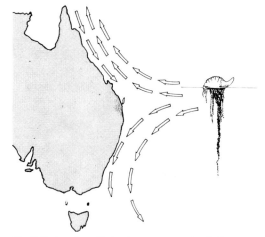

Fig. 18. Eastern Australia showing currents carrying the Portuguese man-of-war, *Physalia*, along Queensland and NSW coastlines.

degrees of virulence, in the outer layer of the body especially in the tentacles, of all polyps and medusae, colonial or solitary. Each nematocyst consists of a fluid-filled capsule containing a long, spirally-coiled, hollow and often barbed, thread (fig. 19). They are used primarily in the capture and stunning of small animals brushing against outstretched tentacles. On appropriate stimulation, and various mechanical and chemical factors are involved here, a change occurs within the capsule; the fluid pressure increases very suddenly and the internally-coiled thread is explosively discharged through one end of the capsule, turning inside-out like the eversion of the finger of a glove. The thread pierces the body of the prey, and on full evagination injects venomous fluid from inside the capsule. Venom from numerous discharged nematocysts rapidly paralyses or kills the victim, which is then drawn by tentacles towards the mouth and swallowed. Once discharged, nema-

Plate 15. A stranded Portuguese man-of-war or bluebottle, *Physalia physalis*.

tocysts are discarded and replaced by new ones formed in special capsule-producing cells.

Both the Portuguese man-of-war, *Physalia physalis*, and the by-the-wind sailor, *Velella lata* (fig. 20 and pl. 17), are normally pelagic (meaning "inhabiting the open sea"), free-floating colonies supported at the surface of the water by a gas-filled float. Though bearing sailing crests and able to move at an angle to the wind, they are almost entirely at the mercy of winds and ocean currents for their distribution. *Physalia*, with float-lengths ranging up to 6 inches or more in Australian waters, and *Velella*, up to about 2 inches across the oval disc, occur in warm waters all over the world. Off eastern Australia, men-of-war and by-the-wind sailors come from the tropical Pacific with the warm South Equatorial Current. Under normal conditions they pass south along the southern Queensland and New South Wales coastline in the East Australian Current, or north along the outer Barrier Reef in the northern branch of the Equatorial Current (fig. 18). Strong and continuous winds drive *Physalia* and *Velella* on to the Queensland and New South Wales beaches, often with other floating pelagic animals, nearly all blue in colour. These include the smaller, sail-less and circular coelenterate, *Porpita pacifica*, and the violet snail, *Janthina janthina* (pl. 38h).

Surf beach strandings, and the associated *Physalia* stinging of bathers, can occur in south-eastern Australia throughout the year, but mass "bluebottle" invasions are more frequent with prevailing onshore summer winds when the East Australian Current flows closer to the coastline.

The float of *Physalia*, together with the numerous short, feeding polyps clustered beneath and the long, trailing, fishing tentacles, are all individual members of the one colony. The float is a modified medusoid form, the tentacles are extensions of modified protective polyps and other polyps are modified for reproduction. The long tentacles are studded with bead-like batteries of nematocysts capable of disabling animals, including fish, as large as the colony itself. In Australian waters these fishing extensions may reach a length of 14 feet or more, but can contract to a few inches in a matter of seconds. It is contact with these heavily-armed tentacles that causes the severe stinging of human bathers so characteristic of a *Physalia* surf invasion. The nematocysts responsible (shown here highly magnified, both undischarged, fig. 19, and discharged, pl. 16), are of two different sizes but are of the same basic structure and function. The nematocyst thread (seen coiled internally in both side and plan views in the black and white photomicrograph),

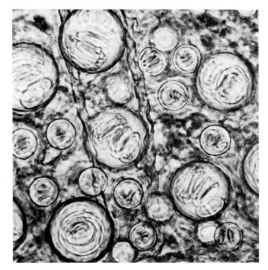

Fig. 19. Photomicrograph of *Physalia* nematocysts, mainly undischarged (approx. x640).

Plate 16. Discharged nematocysts from Portuguese man-of-war (approx. x1040).

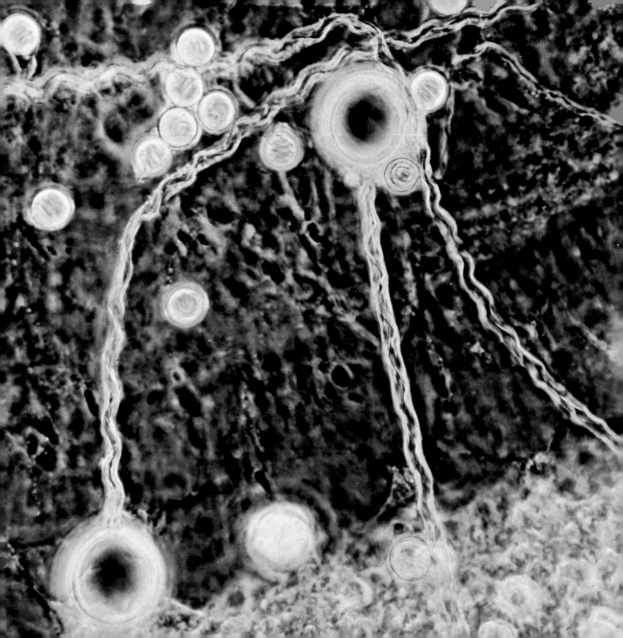

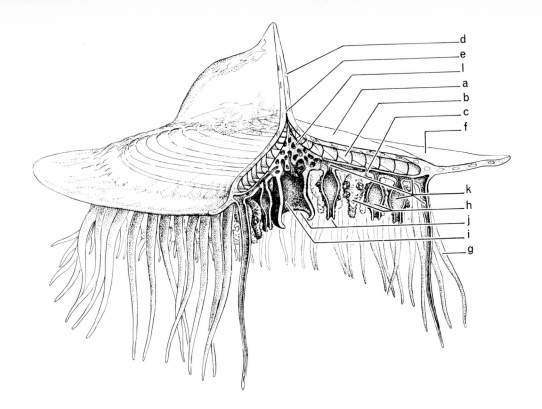

Fig. 20. A by-the-wind sailor, *Velella lata*, with part of colony cut away to show various specialised polyps and structure of float: *a*, float; *b*, concentric chitinous air chambers of float; *c*, chitinous canal from float chamber to lower surface; *d*, sail; *e*, chitinous support for sail; *f*, edge of disc; *g*, stinging tentacular polyp; *h*, reproductive polyps with medusal buds; *i*, central feeding polyp; *j*, open mouths of polyps; *k*, continuous gastrovascular cavity; *l*, liver.

when fully discharged, is of great length and is spirally twisted on itself (as seen in the colour, phase-contrast photomicrograph).

The venom injected by *Physalia* nematocysts appears to contain a complex protein neurotoxin, a pain-producer such as 5-hydroxytryptamine and a paralysing factor, probably a quaternary ammonium base. Coelenterate nematocyst venoms in general are under study by various laboratories around the world, but their detailed composition is still largely unknown. Although stinging by *Physalia* can cause excruciating pain, even collapse in some cases, and often leaves slow-healing, linear marks and weals on the skin, no human deaths have ever been authentically and directly attributed to the Portuguese man-of-war.

Plate 17. A floating by-the-wind sailor, *Velella lata*.

BELLS WITH TENTACLES
jellyfish

THERE ARE THREE MAIN GROUPS of coelenterate animals. There are hydrozoans (typically with both polyp and medusoid forms in their life cycles), which include the sedentary and usually colonial hydroids (fig. 38, growth on shell), the pelagic colonies such as the Portuguese man-of-war, *Physalia*, and the by-the-wind sailor, *Velella*, as well as that rather aberrant little solitary polyp, the freshwater *Hydra*. Then there are scyphozoans (with a medusa as the main or only form in their life cycle), which include the solitary larger jellyfish such as the brown blubber, *Catostylus mosaicus* (pl. 18), and the box-jellies or cubomedusae, including the deadly tropical sea wasps. Finally there are anthozoans (with the polyp as the only form in their life cycle), which include the solitary

Fig. 21. Under-surface of common saucer blubber, *Aurelia aurita*, showing branched radiating canals and central mouth-arms.

sea anemones, such as *Oulactis muscosa* (pl. 21), the alcyonarian soft corals such as *Telesto* (pl. 49, background) and the true or stony corals, both solitary (such as *Balanophyllia bairdiana*, pl. 22) and colonial (such as *Plesiastrea urvillei*, pl. 25).

Jellyfish range in size and complexity from a simple medusa in the life cycle of an intertidal hydroid to the giant scyphozoan medusa, *Cyanea capillata*. The former may be a fraction of an inch across with a single circle of short tentacles, while the latter may grow in the Arctic Ocean up to 7 feet and more in bell diameter, with a multitude of tentacles hanging in a circle of eight bunches and individually ranging up to about 120 feet in length. This same *Cyanea* also occurs in Australian waters, where it is known as the giant blubber. Specimens grey, mauve, pink, or brown in bell colour, and up to about 18 inches to 2 feet across, periodically invade the harbours and beaches of eastern and southern Australia, especially during summer months. The long, trailing tentacles are heavily armed with nematocyst batteries and the giant blubber's sting can be severe and painful. Surf-broken tentacular fragments can cause mass beach stinging, and even nets and lines used at such times pick up and retain these stinging fragments.

The commonest jellyfish in local waters, in fact the commonest in the world, with an almost cosmopolitan distribution, is the saucer blubber or moon jelly, *Aurelia aurita* (fig. 21). At times the estuaries and inlets of south-eastern Australia appear to be virtually swarming with 3 to 9-inch wide, almost transparent, saucer-shaped *Aurelia* and the larger, opaque, bell-shaped brown blubber, *Catostylus* (pl. 18). The former characteristically bears four symmetrically-placed, pinkish reproductive organs within the body, while in the latter these organs are visible from above in the form of a cross.

Plate 18. The brown blubber, *Catostylus mosaicus*, with the alga, *Hormosira*.

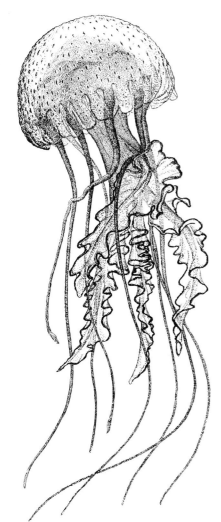

Fig. 22. The mauve stinger, *Pelagia noctiluca.*

In *Catostylus mosaicus* there are no tentacles around the edge of the bell and the central hanging mouth tentacles are fused into 8 thick and grossly-rounded mouth-arms.

Apart from the clogging of fishing nets and power-house intakes by its presence in such vast numbers, *Aurelia* is quite harmless to human beings and can be handled with complete safety at any time. On the other hand, *Catostylus* is a known stinger and, while its effect is not usually severe, contact with nema-tocysts on the mouth-arms can cause local rashes, intense irritation, and nauseating pains.

A beautiful and unusual jellyfish is the delicately-coloured, mauve stinger, *Pelagia noctiluca* (fig. 22). This appears to be a warm water species, which, from time to time and only in certain conditions of wind and current, occurs in swarms along the east coast of Australia. The four frilly mouth-arms and the eight slender tentacles, as well as the nematocyst-bearing warts on the upper surface of the bell, allow immediate identification of this medusa. It reaches a bell diameter of about 5 inches and is a known, but not necessarily severe, stinger. As the scientific name implies, *Pelagia* is capable, like certain other pelagic animals, of producing light.

Though of seasonal occurrence, another charac-teristic jellyfish in the estuaries and inlets of south-eastern Australia is the large and spotted *Phyllorhiza punctata*. A fully grown specimen is shown swim-ming strongly in plate 19 with its bell at the moment of maximum contraction and its long tubular mouth-arms trailing behind. Medusae swim by alternately contracting and relaxing muscle cells in the bell, thereby forcing water rhythmically out of the concave surface and driving the animal in the opposite direction. Orientation and balance of the whole organism is controlled by a series of organs symmetrically placed near the margin of the bell.

Plate 19. The large, estuarine jellyfish, *Phyllorhiza punctata*, actively swimming.

POLYPS AS INDIVIDUALS

sea anemones

SEA ANEMONES are typical polyps: each individual has a stout, muscular body expanded at its upper end into a disc bearing a central mouth surrounded by several circles of hollow tentacles (pl. 20). The lower end of the tubular body is expanded into a muscular, adherent basal disc on which the anemone can creep about slowly and by which it can hold on to rocks and other firm surfaces so tenaciously that one is likely to tear the animal in trying to pry it loose.

From the mouth, a tubular throat, or gullet, hangs down into the gastrovascular cavity and is connected to the body wall by a series of radially-arranged partitions or mesenteries (fig. 23). Between the primary mesenteries, attached to the gullet, are secondary sets of incomplete mesenteries extending only part way from the body wall towards the gullet. The body cavity is thus divided into a series of alcove-like compartments in open communication with one another below the level of the gullet. The mesenteries are infoldings of the lining of the body cavity and thus serve to increase the digestive surface area, making it possible for the anemone to digest a relatively large animal such as an entire crab or a small fish.

The muscular system of an anemone is extensive and co-ordinated by a nerve net, though there is no trace of a brain. A layer of circular muscles serves to narrow, and therefore to extend, the body. Bands of longitudinal muscles pass down mesenteries from mouth disc to basal disc and their contraction can pull the mouth disc and all its tentacles completely inside the body. A circular sphincter muscle just below the mouth disc can then tighten and close the opening, thus protecting an intertidal anemone from drying and damage during exposure at low tide.

Colourful sea anemones are a characteristic feature of most of the world's seashores and Australian shores are no exception. One of the

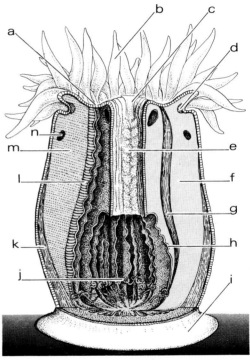

Fig. 23. A sea anemone with part of body cut away to show internal structure: *a,* mouth disc; *b,* tentacle; *c,* mouth; *d,* circular sphincter muscle; *e,* gullet; *f,* primary mesentery; *g,* longitudinal muscle of mesentery; *h,* edge of mesentery; *i,* basal disc; *j,* gastrovascular cavity; *k,* longitudinal muscle at base of mesentery; *l,* reproductive organs on mesentery; *m,* secondary mesentery; *n,* perforation through mesentery.

Plate 20. The anemone, *Telmatactis;* normal light (*left*), ultra-violet (*right*).

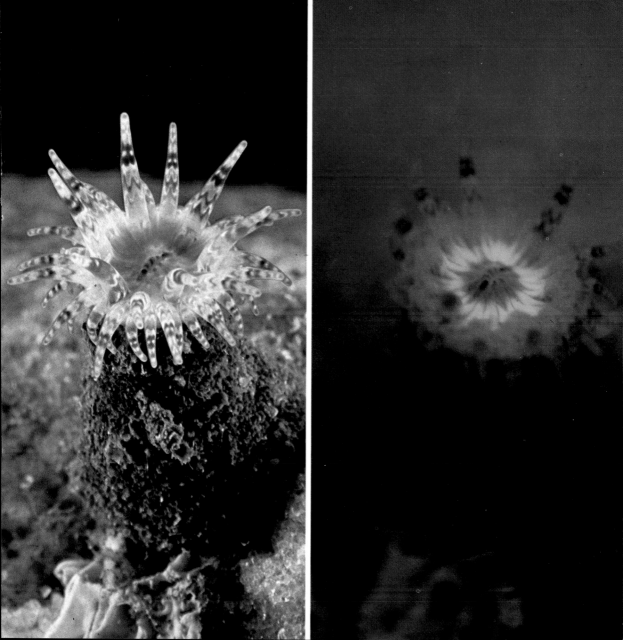

commonest, most conspicuous and widespread of Australian anemones is the sea waratah, *Actinia tenebrosa*, with a smooth, brownish-red body and bright red tentacles. Waratah anemones are usually seen as little, dark, jelly-like blobs exposed at low tide, often crowded together on shaded rock surfaces. At this time their tentacles are withdrawn, but with the return of the tide *Actinia* expands again, revealing the true nature of this little sea "flower".

Some anemones, as well as being distinctively coloured, have the ability to fluoresce, in other words, to glow visibly under ultra-violet light (see next chapter for discussion of this phenomenon). Plate 20 shows a small subtidal species of *Telmatactis* from south-eastern Australia under normal lighting and under ultra-violet illumination. Note the red fluorescence on the mouth disc.

The speckled anemone, *Oulactis muscosa* (pl. 21),

with its inevitable fringe of shell fragments, gravel and sand, is a common intertidal temperate species. It is easily recognised by its dark mouth disc, its pale greenish-grey and often striped tentacles, as well as its constant habit of gathering and attaching to itself assorted inorganic debris. At extreme low water level and below, in New South Wales and Victoria, the little, orange-red Scandinavian itch anemone, *Corynactis australis* (fig. 24), often occurs in great numbers growing together in clumps or in encrusting carpets. It is easily recognised by its distinctive, white-knobbed tentacles, and is regarded by skindivers as a stinger causing mild, though often prolonged, itching. Another stinger is the beautiful, slender-tentacled, orange-yellow *Anthothoe* (back jacket plate) known to skindivers from depths of about 15 to 80 feet off the central New South Wales coast.

Fig. 24. Scandinavian itch anemones, *Corynactis australis.*

Plate 21. Speckled anemones, *Oulactis muscosa*, with the alga, *Corallina.*

POLYPS WITH SKELETONS
corals

A NY COELENTERATE POLYPS, solitary or colonial, which have calcareous skeletons supporting or protecting them are loosely referred to as "corals". Other plant and animal growths are sometimes called "corals", especially the encrusting coralline algae or nullipores, the encrusting *Galeolaria* worm tubes (referred to as "Sydney coral", fig. 3), and the bryozoan sea-mosses and lace-corals (pl. 42). Though all such growths are certainly calcareous and coralline, the use of the term "coral" is considered inappropriate for them and is best restricted to the calcareous coelenterate growths.

Anthozoan corals are broadly divided into two main types according to their structure and appearance: the soft corals, or alcyonarians and the true stony corals, or scleractinians. The soft corals include the horny gorgonians, the sea fans (such as the red, orange or yellow forms of *Mopsella*), the blue coral *Heliopora*, the red organ-pipe coral *Tubipora*, as well as the large, fleshy, soft coral growths of tropical reefs. The antipatharian black corals, whose stems are cut and polished into semi-precious jewellery, form a third and minor group related to the scleractinians.

The polyps of alcyonarian soft corals typically bear eight pinnate, or "feathered", tentacles in contradistinction to the numerous (often in multiples of six) simple tentacles in the stony corals. Even the softest of the alcyonarians has an unsuspected and abundant scattering of complexly-shaped, calcareous spicules within its tissue, and it is this skeleton that shows the close general relationship of the alcyonarians to the scleractinians.

The characteristic colours of alcyonarian skeletons, including blues, reds and yellows, are caused by differing complex iron salts bound into the predominantly calcium carbonate structure. Such permanent colours contrast strongly with the pure white skeletons of most cleaned stony corals. In all scleractinians the characteristic colours of the living corals are confined entirely to their tissue and disappear once the corals are removed from the sea and the polyp flesh has died and decayed. These colours are in fact usually caused by single-celled symbiotic algae, called zooxanthellae, living within the coral tissue. In a few atypical corals the skeleton itself is coloured as can be seen in the temperate Australian *Astrangia* shown in fig. 26. This subtidal coral grows in small encrusting colonies; the skeleton is dark purplish-blue while the living polyp is almost transparent, with some internal green colouring (pl. 23).

A true coral polyp is very similar in general structure to a sea anemone, but is supported by a calcareous cup, or corallite (fig. 27), secreted by the

Fig. 25. Skeleton of solitary cup coral, *Balanophyllia bairdiana.*

Plate 22. Polyp of solitary coral, *Balanophyllia bairdiana.*

polyp itself. From the wall of this external skeletal cup a series of radially arranged, calcareous septa project inwards as thin vertical plates (fig. 25). These septa alternate with the similarly arranged digestive mesenteries in the gastrovascular cavity. Although usually extended well beyond the corallite when relaxed and feeding, the individual polyp is capable of contraction and complete withdrawal into this protective cup when disturbed.

Stony corals, both solitary and colonial, can grow at any depth in the sea and in water of any temperature from the tropics to the polar regions. However, reef-building corals, consisting of those colonial corals with symbiotic zooxanthellae, do not usually grow in water less than about 18 degrees C and in depths greater than about 150 feet. Optimum conditions for reef growth are shallow tropical waters above about 22 degrees C; there, colonial corals reach their greatest development with individual staghorn or brain coral colonies reaching many feet across. The minute polyps of such colonies are linked together over the surface by a thin layer of living tissue.

The Great Barrier Reef of Australia, in all its complexity, is by far the largest structure built by living organisms, animal or plant, anywhere in the world either in the present or at any time in the geological past. Its area has been estimated at 80,000 square miles and it stretches over 1,200 miles from Torres Strait in the north to the scattered island groups off Gladstone, Queensland, in the south. Scleractinian corals are the prime factor in the formation of this huge structure but organisms other than corals are essential for the process of reef consolidation. Thus encrusting calcareous algae, jointed coralline seaweeds such as *Halimeda* and calcareous tests of single-celled foraminiferans in their millions, all contribute towards the formation and maintenance of the Barrier Reef.

About 350 species of stony corals have been recorded from the Great Barrier Reef and this represents about half the total number of scleractinians known from the entire Indo-Pacific area. This great diversity of corals, however, does not extend uniformly down the length of the Barrier Reef. The coral fauna as a whole remains fairly constant in numbers from the northern areas southwards for nearly 800 miles to the vicinity of the Whitsunday Group. Further south there is a rapid decline in the number of coral species present on the Reef, until at Heron Island, near the southern extremity, there is a coral fauna of about 90 recorded species. Coral numbers are further reduced drastically in the temperate waters of eastern Australia, with about 24 species known from Moreton Bay and only about 14 known from as far south as Sydney.

The two common reef-building type corals from the central New South Wales coast are *Plesiastrea urvillei* with bright green or pale bluish-green polyps and tissue (pl. 25 and fig. 29), and *Cos-*

Fig. 26. Corallites of temperate colonial coral, *Astrangia* species.

Plate 23. Polyp of temperate coral, *Astrangia* species.

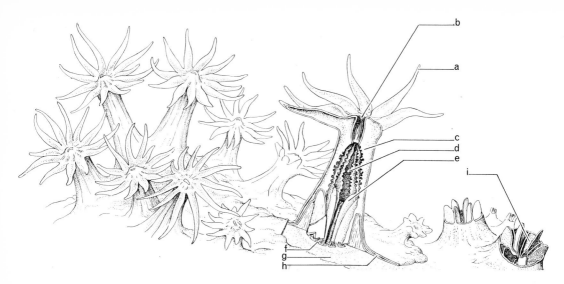

Fig. 27. A coral colony and an individual polyp with part of body cut away to show internal structure: *a*, tentacle; *b*, mouth; *c*, mesentery; *d*, gastrovascular cavity; *e*, septum; *f*, septa cut away; *g*, calcareous skeleton of colony; *h*, tissue linking adjacent polyps; *i*, calcareous cup or corallite, without polyp.

cinaraea mcneilli with brown polyps. Both are subtidal and grow in great encrusting sheets over rock surfaces or over dead coral from shallow water down to a depth of about 60 feet.

There are four, non-reef-building corals reasonably abundant in eastern warm temperate intertidal and shallow waters. These are all modest growths, solitary or in small colonial groupings, without symbiotic zooxanthellae in their tissues, and without the strict temperature and other environmental requirements of most reef-building corals. The smallest and simplest is *Culicia quinarea*, a solitary, orange-polyped form with a one-quarter-inch wide corallite cup, often found growing in close clusters on the under surface of intertidal stone slabs. Another solitary and beautiful cup coral is *Balanophyllia bairdiana* (pl. 22 and fig. 25) which occurs

Fig. 28. Corallites of temperate colonial coral, *Dendrophyllia* species.

Plate 24. Polyps of temperate coral, *Dendrophyllia* species. ⇩

on rock bottoms from depths of about 20 feet down to several hundred feet. Its straight-walled corallite varies from about half an inch to one inch in width and may be somewhat flattened from side to side when growing in crowded conditions.

The delicate and strikingly beautiful *Astrangia* (pl. 23), with its coloured corallites, has been mentioned already. The rather irregularly-formed colonies (fig. 26) are seldom more than an inch or two across and can be found growing from just below tidal level to a depth of 20 feet or more. A similar, though somewhat larger and more compact colonial coral, is the species of *Dendrophyllia* shown in plate 24 and fig. 28. It appears to have very nearly the same depth range as *Balanophyllia* and grows under the same conditions.

Fluorescent colours in living corals, as in sea anemones (pl. 20), can be striking and dramatic. Plate 25 shows the same area of the common, temperate *Plesiastrea urvillei* under normal lighting

Fig. 29. Skeleton of colonial coral, *Plesiastrea urvillei.*

and under ultra-violet illumination. Although not as intense as that shown by some tropical corals, the blue fluorescence of this normally green *Plesiastrea* is relatively bright and provides a fine display in a demonstration aquarium. *Coscinaraea mcneilli* is, however, apparently not fluorescent.

Although previously observed by others the unexpectedly varied and bright fluorescent colours of certain deep-water corals was first demonstrated on a large scale by Dr René Catala at the Noumea Aquarium, New Caledonia, in 1957. Fluorescence is the ability to glow visibly under ultra-violet light (which itself is invisible to the human eye) and contrasts with luminescence, or phosphorescence as it is sometimes called, which is the ability to glow, or produce light, quite independently of any external illumination or irradiation (as in the worm *Chaetopterus*, pl. 29).

Dr Catala obtained his many species of fluorescent corals from depths of about 70 to 150 feet, both within the lagoon and on the outer slope of the New Caledonian barrier reef. In his book *Carnival Under the Sea* Catala provides many colour photographs of these corals fluorescing and makes several general comments on this phenomenon. He found that only a limited number of species respond to ultra-violet radiation; that only the living flesh of the coral could fluoresce, not the calcareous skeleton; that the fluorescence was independent of the symbiotic zooxanthellae within the coral tissue, and that overexposure to ultra-violet rays brought about a decrease in the intensity of fluorescence. Several different fluorescent pigments have been identified from these corals (compounds related to flavines, urobilines and pterines), but as yet no satisfactory physiological reason for this fluorescence, or any possible use of this phenomenon by the corals themselves, has been put forward.

Plate 25. *Plesiastrea urvillei;* normal light (*left*), ultra-violet (*right*).

VORACIOUS TUBES
marine worms

Many different animal groups are loosely called "worms". Though it is convenient to deal with several of these groups under the one heading, this does not imply that they are closely related. Worms in general are soft-bodied, bilaterally symmetrical animals, usually with a distinct head or front end, and usually, but not always, elongated and capable of reasonably active movements. All but some parasitic forms have a mouth and tubular gut, and many are carnivorous.

On Australian seashores four groups of marine worms are commonly seen. These are the platyhelminth flatworms (related to parasitic flukes and tapeworms), the nemertean ribbon-worms, the annelid polychaete worms (cylindrical, segmented animals related to earthworms) and the sipunculoid peanut-worms. The polychaetes are by far the most abundant and important of all the marine worms and will be considered first.

Annelid worms (including both the terrestrial earthworms and the marine polychaetes) typically possess segmented bodies and a series of bristles, or setae, projecting through the skin of each

Fig. 30. Pulling giant beach-worm from sand in one firm and continuous movement.

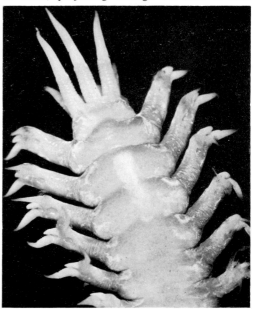

Fig. 31. Head and anterior segments of giant beach-worm, *Onuphis teres*, showing parapodia.

Plate 26. Luring and catching giant beach-worm, *Onuphis teres.*

segment. In addition, polychaetes usually have a well-defined head, often with eyes and tentacles, and each segment of the body bears a muscular flap or extension on each side. These flaps are called parapodia (fig. 31) and are variously used in different species as digging organs, legs, or swimming paddles. The parapodia may bear gills and in many species their movements aid respiration.

One of the largest polychaetes in the Australian area is the giant beach-worm, *Onuphis teres* (pl. 26 and fig. 31), which reaches a length of 8 feet or more. *Onuphis* is a common burrower in the sand of many open surf beaches in Queensland, New South Wales and South Australia, but is not often seen unless specially searched for. It is a well-known and, when sold commercially, highly-priced bait worm, usually sought and captured by a specialised technique requiring considerable skill.

The beach-worms live completely buried in the sand where the surf breaks at low tide level. The expert worm-catcher trails a piece of smelly fish or other dead animal as a lure over the sand in the shallow back-wash of the waves. Sensing the lure in the moving water, nearby *Onuphis* pop their heads out of the sand for an instant in an attempt to locate this desirable food. The momentary emergence of a head causes a V-shaped ripple in the back-wash and thus gives away the position of the worm. Moving to the spot where a head appeared, the catcher touches the sand with a small piece of bait, often a crushed shellfish, held in one hand. Usually the head reappears and the worm grabs the bait in its jaws. With the other hand the catcher seizes the worm just below the head at the surface of the sand and firmly but smoothly pulls the animal out in one continuous movement. This is when skill is required, as a hesitation at this stage, or too vigorous a pull, and the worm will grip the

Fig. 32. The bristle-worm, *Eurythoe complanata*, a well-known temperate and tropical stinger.

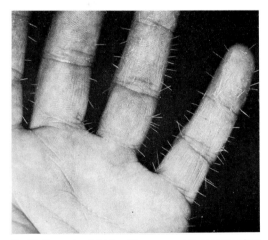

Fig. 33. Human hand thistly with numerous detached setae of the bristle-worm, *Eurythoe*.

Plate 27. The iridescent scale-worm, *Lepidonotus melanogrammus*.

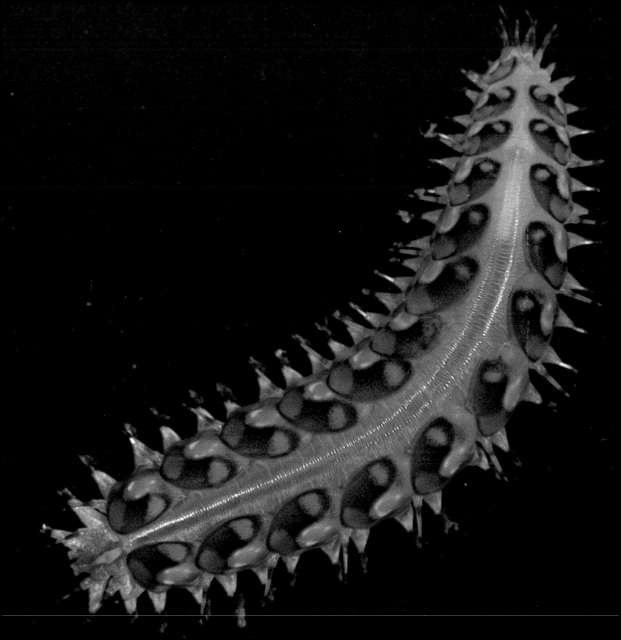

Fig. 34. Tropical tube-worm with beautiful pale crown of gill plumes.

the projecting portions, which cause the stinging reaction. *Eurythoe*, cream-coloured in tropical waters but pink on temperate shores, grows to about 7 inches and is found on rocky beaches under stones, among coral rubble, or within narrow crevices.

The scale-worm, *Lepidonotus melanogrammus* (pl. 27), is a beautifully-patterned polychaete, reasonably common under intertidal stones in temperate waters. The brown tones of the paired segmental scales and the glistening setae on the parapodia, as seen in the colour photograph, provide a pleasing contrast to the iridescent blue of the exposed upper surface of the worm. The scales themselves are easily detached from the body of *Lepidonotus*, and if seen loose and unassociated often puzzle the uninitiated as to their origin.

In those polychaetes which live permanently in a self-made tube or burrow the body is often con-

Fig. 35. Outer surface of operculum or lid of plumed tube-worm, *Serpula vermicularis*.

sand with its parapodia and will break. In plate 26 the lure is the dead ray in the water behind the catcher, while the hand-bait is a pipi in his left hand. Both this photograph, and that in fig. 30, show a catcher in the act of pulling worms out of the sand in one firm and continuous movement.

Another notable polychaete is the almost world-wide, warm-water, intertidal bristle-worm, *Eurythoe complanata* (fig. 32), well-known to biologists and marine collectors in Australia and many other parts of the world on account of its painful stinging. As the common name suggests, the numerous setae of this particular worm are large and project in bunches from each side of the body in a continuous fringe. Unlike the setae of most polychaetes those of *Eurythoe* are slender, rigid and brittle slivers, composed mainly of calcium carbonate. These stick into the fingers and then break off, to remain closely-spaced, but irregularly-placed, like a partly-filled pincushion (fig. 33). It is these setae, or the fragments embedded in the skin after removal of

Plate 28. The tube-worm, *Serpula vermicularis*, partially expanded.

siderably modified, with the anterior end usually specialised for tube-building, feeding, and respiration. A common, though individually small, example of this group is the tube-worm *Galeolaria*, whose encrusting calcareous tubes (fig. 3) are so characteristic of the warm temperate region. Another temperate species, almost world-wide in distribution, is the red plumed tube-worm, *Serpula vermicularis* (pl. 28), found under stones on rocky coasts. In an undisturbed state a crown of spirally-arranged gill plumes and a radially-ribbed operculum, or lid (fig. 35), project from the mouth of the firm, limy tube. These brightly-coloured plumes, often brilliantly red in this species, form a complex breathing and food-catching apparatus which can be rapidly withdrawn into the tube at the least disturbance. The operculum, vase-shaped in side view, closes the entrance to the tube at such times. Figure 34 shows a beautifully plumed tropical tube-worm, with a half-inch diameter, creamy-white crown.

Undoubtedly the most unusual and fascinating of all the animals mentioned in this book is the extraordinary parchment-tube worm, *Chaetopterus variopedatus*, already referred to on page 22. The estuarine habitat and "innkeeping" habits of this specialised polychaete are shown in plate 8 and fig. 9, while the complex shape and external features are shown in colour and diagrammatically in plate 29 and fig. 36. When removed from its U-shaped tube, *Chaetopterus* is found to have a short, clearly segmented head region followed by an attenuated middle section, bearing two wing-shaped food-collecting flaps, a dark liver mass and three

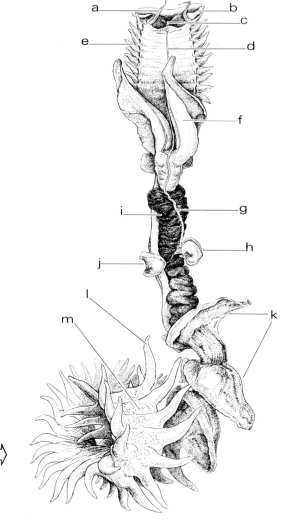

Fig. 36. The parchment-tube worm, *Chaetopterus variopedatus*, removed from tube to show external features: *a*, tentacle; *b*, "lip"; *c*, mouth; *d*, food groove; *e*, parapodium; *f*, wing-shaped flap (modified 12th parapod); *g*, dorsal ciliated food groove; *h*, dorsal food cup; *i*, liver; *j*, ventral adhesive sucker; *k*, fans (modified 14th-16th parapodia); *l*, enlarged parapodial process; *m*, pink convoluted ovary.

Plate 29. Luminescent photo-image of *Chaetopterus* (*right*), normal light (*left*).

Fig. 37. Orange and black-banded flatworm, *Pseudoceros corallophilus*, from tropical reef waters.

If a specimen is removed from its tube and examined alive in the dark, certain parts of the body will glow brightly under the stimulus of a touch, a sudden knock or a slight electric shock. A unique photograph of this phenomenon is given here (pl. 29, *right*), taken in colour, and using only the light produced by the worm itself. We believe that this is the first colour photograph of *Chaetopterus* luminescence to be published.

The light given out by the parchment-tube worm is a cold light, that is, light produced with almost no loss of energy as heat. The chemistry of bioluminescence (light produced by living organisms) is by no means fully understood, but it has been found that in the case of *Chaetopterus* it is due to the reaction of a special protein with oxygen, in the presence of certain iron salts and traces of other complex compounds. Excess energy, a mere byproduct of this reaction, is given off as light. Whether these worms luminesce when undisturbed within their tubes (they cannot leave their tubes at any time under natural conditions) is not known.

large fans. Finally an elongated tail section, curled on itself in the colour plate and figure, bears numerous, enlarged parapodial processes. Under natural conditions the worm fits loosely within its tube, and maintains, by the rhythmical beating of its three fans, a current of water passing from the narrow entrance "straw" through to the equally narrow exit. Food particles contained in this water are filtered out as the current passes through a bag of mucus secreted by the worm and suspended between the two separated wing-shaped flaps and the dorsal food cup. As the bag is continuously formed by the wing flaps, the food-filled posterior portion is rolled up within the food cup. Periodically mucous balls pass forwards to the mouth along the dorsal ciliated food groove. When feeding, the worm holds its position within the tube by using several ventral suckers (only one visible in plate).

Chaetopterus is one of those unusual and exciting animals which have the ability to luminesce, that is, to produce their own light, apparently at will.

The strikingly-coloured flatworm shown in fig. 37 is one of the "magic carpet" turbellarians from tropical waters. Its name, *Pseudoceros corallophilus*, refers not only to its coral reef habitat but also to the characteristic horn-like, tentacular flaps at the front of the body. In life, the opaque, wafer-thin animal is creamy-white with vividly-contrasting marginal bands of rich orange-brown and intense black, with an extreme outer edging of bright yellow. The small, orange-red ribbon-worm, *Gorgonorhynchus repens* (pl. 30), is very much the exception among its nemertean relatives. Its proboscis, a characteristic feeding and defensive organ in this group of worms, is seen to be multi-branched when protruded. In all other ribbon-worms this organ is narrow, elongate, and unbranched.

Plate 30. The small ribbon-worm, *Gorgonorhynchus repens*, with protruded proboscis.

SHELLS AND JOINTED FEET
crustaceans

INSECTS AND CRUSTACEANS both belong to the same general group, the arthropods or "jointed-feet" animals. The tremendous diversification, abundance, and what one might call the biological success of this great group is due in large part to the development of the outer body layer, or cuticle, into a protective armour. This armour, the "crust" or shell part of the word crustacean, is non-living and is secreted by the underlying tissue. In whole or in part it forms outer protective coverings, biting jaws, grinding surfaces, eye lenses, tactile sense organs, sound-producing organs, walking legs, nippers, swimming paddles and other structures.

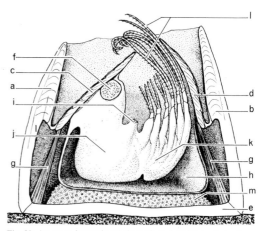

Fig. 39. An acorn barnacle cut through to show internal structure. *a-e*, shell plates; *a*, rostrum; *b*, carina; *c*, scutum; *d*, tergum; *e*, shell base; *f*, adductor muscle (cut section); *g*, retractor muscle; *h*, mantle cavity; *i*, mouth; *j*, region of stomach; *k*, thorax; *l*, cirri; *m*, ovary.

There are several layers in the arthropod cuticle and, depending on the characteristic habits and habitat of the particular animals examined, these contain differing amounts of waterproofing wax, flexible chitin, and rigid calcium carbonate. This rigid armour, or exoskeleton, acts as a supporting framework for the tissues within and for the attachment of muscles. Between areas of inflexible hardening, the cuticle remains as a flexible membrane or joint, thus allowing mobility as well as protection. In order to grow, an arthropod must periodically shed, or moult, its outermost layers of cuticle. Underneath these the animal already possesses a newly-formed and larger cuticular sheath, which remains elastic, or "soft-shelled", for a short period at each moult to allow for a small amount of growth.

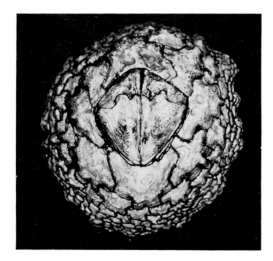

Fig. 38. One of the surf-barnacles, *Catophragmus polymerus*, with its many shell-plates.

Plate 31. Stranded, pelagic goose barnacles, *Lepas anserifera*.

Fig. 40. The shore slater, *Ligia australiensis*, a fast-moving intertidal scavenger.

Crustaceans may be distinguished from other arthropods by their possession of gills and, though some subgroups have terrestrial representatives, the majority are aquatic. Freshwater members abound, but the group is predominantly marine and is so abundant in the oceans that crustaceans have sometimes been called the "insects of the sea".

Without considering here the small planktonic crustaceans such as the copepods (pl. 13), the simplest and perhaps the most abundant members of the group on Australian seashores are the barnacles. Looking very much like molluscan shellfish, with their thick calcareous plates and their invariable attachment to some fixed or free-moving object, barnacles are, however, true crustacean arthropods as can be seen from their structure and life history. Their limbs, or cirri, are jointed (fig. 39), and their early larval stages have appendages and a median eye, just as do those of other crustaceans.

There are two main types of barnacles: the acorn or sessile barnacles and the goose or stalked barnacles. The former are especially common firmly attached to intertidal rocks or mangrove roots and have been mentioned already in connection with zonation (fig. 6). Examples of the latter can be found washed ashore, attached by a flexible stalk to a log or some other floating object. Some intertidal acorn barnacles have an external wall of only four plates and a shell aperture closed by two pairs of valves. At the other extreme in plate number is the wide-ranging surf-barnacle, *Catophragmus polymerus* (fig. 38), with eight main wall plates and numerous smaller, overlapping accessory plates.

The most commonly-seen goose barnacle is *Lepas anserifera* (pl. 31), with its characteristically short stalk. It occurs, as does the closely-related, long-stalked *Lepas anatifera*, in all tropical seas and is a true oceanic drifter. Both species can be found attached to a variety of floating objects such as corks, pumice, wreckage, logs of wood or even to other pelagic animals such as the molluscs *Janthina* and *Recluzia* (pl. 36, small *Lepas* on spire of shell).

Variously named shore slaters, gribbles, fish-lice, and sand-hoppers, there is a group of small crustaceans with a wide range of form and habits, including that of timber destruction. These are the isopods and amphipods. The former are flattened from above downwards and in consequence move readily in the usual manner on several pairs of legs (for example the shore slater, *Ligia*, fig. 40); the latter are compressed from side to side and often move by a series of jumps or hops (for example the beach sand-hopper, *Orchestia*). Many of the isopods are parasitic, especially in fish, and damage to wooden structures in the sea by timber-boring isopods, like *Limnoria* and *Sphaeroma*, and amphipods, for example *Chelura*, is a major economic problem in many Australian harbours.

Plate 32. The common, commercial king prawn, *Penaeus plebejus*.

Balancing the problems posed by the destructive activities of certain smaller crustaceans is the economic value of several larger forms—the prawns, crayfish, and crabs. These larger forms all belong to a major crustacean group called the decapods. As the name signifies, members of this group all have ten legs, arranged in five similarly-sized pairs, as in most prawns, or in one pair of enlarged nippers and four pairs of walking legs, as in most crabs. Hermit-crabs, with their soft, spirally-twisted abdomens, or tails, form a rather intermediate division between the straight-bodied shrimps, prawns, and crayfish, and the round or square-shaped true crabs, with their abdomens reduced and folded forwards under the combined head and thorax.

The head and part of the thorax of the commercial king prawn of eastern Australia, *Penaeus plebejus*, seen in plate 32, shows several of the features typical of the unspecialised, straight-bodied decapods. These are the elongate and narrow body shape, the large, many-faceted eyes on stalks, the long tactile feelers, or antennae (folded back in this photograph), and the slender, rather delicate legs, armed in some cases with simple nippers. An exceptional feature separating prawns of this type (penaeid prawns) from all other decapods, is the fact that they shed their eggs directly into the sea after fertilization. Shrimps, crayfish, hermit-crabs and true crabs all carry their eggs about with them until they hatch. The eggs are characteristically attached to swim-merets under the tail, and females in this condition are said to be in berry, or berried.

Alpheus pacificus (fig. 41), one of the many tropical and temperate snapping shrimps, is a typical egg-carrying decapod, whose small size and lack of a prominent projecting rostrum between the eyes qualifies it for the general name shrimp, rather than prawn. Snapping, or pistol, shrimps are capable of producing a loud and sharp crack, very like the crack of breaking glass, with their enlarged hand. The first pair of legs are modified into strong nippers in these shrimps and one member of the pair is invariably much larger than the other. This big hand has a peg-like projection on the movable finger of the nipper which fits into a socket on the fixed finger. The sudden closing of these fingers under strong muscular tension, like the triggered release of a gun hammer, produces a snapping sound as the peg goes into the socket. This sound-producing mechanism, and the associated jet of water, appears to be used in both offence and defence by these little shrimps.

The banded coral shrimp, *Stenopus hispidus* (pl. 33), is a colourful and extraordinary animal found throughout the tropical waters of the Indian and Pacific Oceans, and in the West Indies. It lives in

Fig. 41. A tropical snapping shrimp, *Alpheus pacificus*, with enlarged sound-producing hand.

Plate 33. The banded coral shrimp, *Stenopus hispidus*.

Fig. 42. Red flapjack or squat crayfish, *Arctides antipodarum*, from shallow south-eastern waters.

coral or rock crevices and in underwater caves from low tide level right down through the depths usually visited by skindivers. In Australia, it is known to occur from about North West Cape in Western Australia, around the northern and north-eastern coasts, south to Shellharbour in southern New South Wales. It has been observed that the banded coral shrimp has the unusual habit of cleaning fish, a form of behaviour shown by only a few tropical shrimps and some tropical fish. Pairs of *Stenopus* have been observed in coral crevices with their feelers projecting and displayed in the sunlight. Fish are attracted to these waving white antennae (six branches to each animal) and remain still while the shrimp picks with its two pairs of small nippers (it does not use the large banded pair for cleaning) at parasites, injured tissue and fungal growths on their bodies and fins. The shrimp does not leave its crevice to clean, but merely reaches out towards the fish, which appear to congregate around known *Stenopus* cleaning sites.

The two best-known Australian marine crayfish, and the largest, are found off the south-eastern and southern coasts. These are the eastern crayfish, *Jasus verreauxi*, and the southern crayfish, *Jasus novaehollandiae*. Giant proportions are reached by the former in the temperate waters along the New South Wales coast; it can weigh at least 17 pounds and be 3 feet in length, excluding the feelers. In Western Australia an important export trade has developed based on another species, the western crayfish, *Panulirus cygnus*.

The terms lobster and crayfish are used haphazardly in Australia to describe these edible crustaceans. The question as to which of the two names is more appropriate is often a source of doubt and argument. There are in fact no lobsters fished commercially in the Southern Hemisphere. The large commercial crustaceans fished in Australian waters belong to an entirely different grouping of decapods from the North Atlantic lobsters. Furthermore, they do not possess the lobster's characteristic large and powerful grasping claws on the first pair of legs. The Australian animals should be referred to as "marine crayfish" to avoid confusion with the equally well-known "freshwater crayfish". The latter possess a pair of big claws, and thus would appear at first sight to be closer to the true northern lobster than to our marine crayfish. However, they belong to another and different grouping again. Other marine crayfish-like animals are the flapjacks, or squat crayfish, of temperate and

Plate 34. The red bait crab, *Plagusia chabrus*.

tropical waters. Figure 42 shows the south-eastern squat crayfish, *Arctides antipodarum*, occasionally seen by skindivers in shallow rocky waters.

The crab fauna of Australia is large and varied. At least 600 species have been recognised from this area and probably many more, especially small and commensal crabs, await discovery. Some idea of their range in form and habits can be gathered from the variety of descriptive terms used in combination with the word "crab". Common names such as sponge crab, spider, camouflage, swimming, mud, ghost (fig. page 9), sand-bubbler (fig. 7), fiddler, semaphore (fig. 10), sentinel, bait (pl. 34), reef, rock (fig. 43), soldier (pl. 35), marsh and shore crabs give an indication of the number and richness of these decapods on our shores.

Perhaps the most unusual, and certainly one of the most spectacular, of all the Australian crabs is the gregarious soldier crab, *Mictyris longicarpus*. This wide-spread temperate and tropical species, and its two close Australian relatives, are well-known in popular literature for their habit of forming large aggregations, or armies, of individuals on sandy tidal flats during low tide (pl. page 5 and

Fig. 44. An army of soldier crabs, *Mictyris longicarpus*, moving over *Zostera* flat.

fig. 44). A predictable sequence of events precedes the formation of armies. As the tide recedes, the smooth surface of the flat becomes broken by eruptions of tumbled sand, occasional individuals emerge, then suddenly large numbers of crabs appear on the previously empty scene. Unlike the familiar sideways movements of other crabs, the soldiers begin to walk forwards towards the water, feeding on surface organic fragments, and leaving behind pear-shaped sand pellets as they move. Gradually they form into small groups and, as feeding diminishes, these groups merge into armies containing, on occasion, thousands of individuals. Such aggregations may commonly wander distances as great as 500 yards. As the tide returns, the soldier crabs move towards the upper levels of the flats, break formation and begin to go down into the sand again. Their rapid and distinctive burrowing could be described as corkscrewing their way into the sand, as they dig down with the legs on one side while walking backwards with the legs on the other.

Fig. 43. Swift-footed rock crab or steelback, *Leptograpsus variegatus*, from temperate shores.

Plate 35. An individual soldier crab, *Mictyris longicarpus*.

EIGHT, TWO, ONE OR NONE
molluscs

SNAILS, SLUGS, OYSTERS, pipis, octopuses and squids all belong to the same major invertebrate grouping, the Mollusca, or "soft-bodied" animals. Despite the lack of similarity in their general external appearance, the body plan is fundamentally the same and differs significantly from those of all other invertebrate groupings. The common name "shellfish", often used for these animals, can be misleading as some (sea-slugs and octopuses) have no shell at all, while others can have one, two or eight separate shells.

There are five major molluscan groups: three are large and well known—the gastropods or univalves, the pelecypods or bivalves, and the cephalopods (octopuses and squids); while two are smaller and not well known—the scaphopods or tusk shells (a very small group, containing *Dentalium*, pl. 37e) and the amphineurans or chitons (fig. 45). The latter, sometimes called coat-of-mail shells, are usually regarded as the least specialised of these five groups.

Chitons are slow-moving animals, usually found on intertidal or immediately subtidal rocks, and when disturbed they are capable of clamping down on the rock surface so tightly that they cannot be moved without damage. The body is bilaterally symmetrical and the ventral surface is largely made up of a broad, flattened, muscular foot (fig. 47) on which the animal creeps. Above the foot is the digestive system, or gut, extending from the mouth, through a simple stomach, to the anus. Immediately inside the mouth there is a muscular pharynx containing a unique and characteristic molluscan organ, the radula. This is an ever-growing, horny ribbon covered with innumerable rows of small curved teeth. When the chiton is feeding, the radula protrudes through the mouth and rasps algae from the underlying rock surface. The gut is covered from above by a fold of tissue which extends along both sides of the foot. This fold is the mantle and the space on each side of the foot, containing a row of gills, is called the mantle cavity. On its upper surface the mantle secretes the shell, which in chitons usually consists of eight calcareous plates overlapping one another like a suit of armour. Around the outer margins of these plates there is a muscular flap, or girdle, often bearing calcareous spicules or minute scales. Figure 45 shows the common, snake's skin chiton, *Sypharochiton pelliserpentis*, its descriptive name based on the appearance of these girdle scales.

The gastropods, or univalves, are a large and varied group with many thousands of representa-

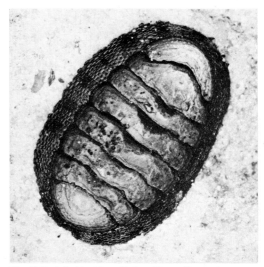

Fig. 45. Snake's skin chiton, *Sypharochiton pelliserpentis*, common in the south-eastern intertidal.

Plate 36. The pelagic snail, *Recluzia rollandiana*, with egg float.

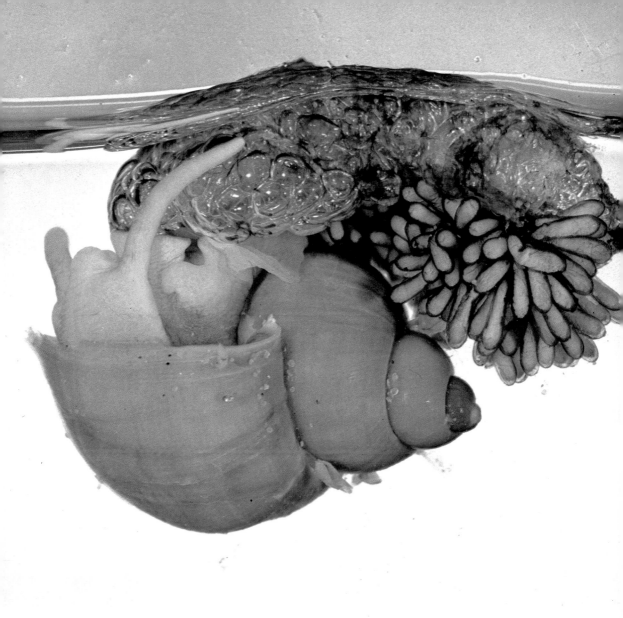

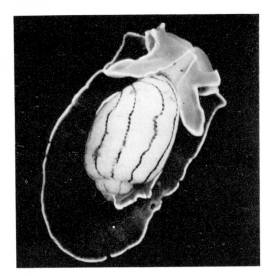

Fig. 46. Lined bubble shell, *Bullina lineata*, with expanded mantle, head tentacles, and eyes.

tives living in Australia. They range in size from the false trumpet shell of northern Australia, which grows to a length of almost 2 feet, down to minute species about the size of a small pin head. The shell is usually external (fig. 47) and coiled in a clockwise (opening on the right) spiral, though sinistrally coiled shells do occasionally occur. In some forms, such as the limpets (pl. 37c), the external shell is not coiled at all but is simple and cap-shaped.

Plate 37. Key to opposite page:

(a) *Decorisepia rex*—royal cuttle (Terrigal, NSW).
(b) *Cypraea (Erosaria) labrolineata*—Nash's cowry (Minnie Waters, near Grafton, NSW).
(c) *Patellanax perplexa*—star limpet (Sydney, NSW).
(d) *Spirula spirula*—ramshorn squid (Bawley Point, near Ulladulla, NSW).

(e) *Dentalium lubricatum*—orange tusk shell (off Sydney).
(f) *Gazameda gunnii*—Gunn's screw shell (off Sydney).
(g) *Opalia australis*—Australian wentletrap (Port Fairy, Vic).
(h) *Phasianotrochus eximius*—true kelp shell (SE Australia).
(i) *Mimelenchus ventricosus*—common pheasant shell (Long Reef, near Sydney).
(j) *Bullina lineata*—lined bubble shell (Pelsart Is, WA).
(k) *Poropteron angasi*—Angas's murex, 2 examples (Sydney).
(l) *Bankivia fasciata*—banded kelp shell (Sydney).
(m) *Hinea brasiliana*—yellow clusterwink (Sydney).
(n) *Austrocochlea obtusa*—common periwinkle (Two-fold Bay, NSW).
(o) *Notohaliotis ruber*—Sydney ear shell (Sydney).
(p) *Morula marginalba*—mulberry whelk (Moreton Bay, Qld).
(q) *Nodilittorina pyramidalis*—tuberculated noddiwink (Jervis Bay, NSW).
(r) *Nodopelagia brazieri*—Brazier's buccinum (Minnie Waters, NSW).

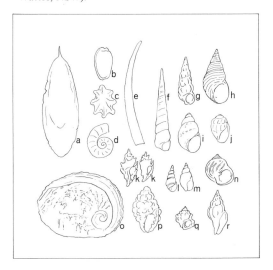

Other forms have a rudimentary, partly coiled, or partly internal shell; some have a completely internal shell, while a large group (pl. 39) has no trace of a shell. Many gastropods have a horny or calcareous door to the shell (pl. 38p). This operculum, as it is termed, is normally attached to the foot, but if found separately from its shell, a calcareous operculum is called a cat's-eye.

The variety of forms included in the gastropods is outstanding. Nearly all the most beautiful and highly-prized molluscan shells belong to this group. Plates 37 and 38 show temperate representatives of many different gastropod forms, the species chosen being reasonably common and generally in the condition in which they are picked up on southern Australian seashores. The volutes, cowries and cones are represented by well-known temperate species, as are the murex shells and wentletraps. Other forms such as screw, kelp and pheasant shells; periwinkles, abalones (pl. 37o), whelks and turban shells; helmets, mitres and purples, are all examples of large and widely distributed gastropod families. The delicate, lined bubble shell, *Bullina lineata*, is shown both alive, with its expanded and brilliantly blue-edged mantle, and as an empty shell (fig. 46 and pl. 37j).

Nudibranchs, or "naked-gill" gastropods, and their allies form a rather distinct group on their own, almost all breathtakingly beautiful if seen alive and almost all with shapes and colours impossible to preserve. A shell is usually present in the larval stage but is lost soon after hatching. The animals are slug-like in shape, elongate or rounded,

Plate 38. Key to opposite page:

(a) *Monoplex australasiae*—hairy whelk, denuded specimen (Seal Rocks, NSW).
(b) *Ninella torquata*—Sydney turban (Geographe Bay, WA).
(c) *Cypraea (Ravitrona) caputserpentis*—serpent's head cowry (Long Reef, near Sydney, NSW).
(d) *Nassarius particeps*—Sydney dog whelk (Sydney).
(e) *Conus (Floraconus) papilliferus*—papillated cone (Sydney).
(f) *Xenogalea labiata*—agate helmet (Wooli, NSW).
(g) *Dicathais orbita*—cart-rut shell (Huskisson, NSW).
(h) *Janthina janthina*—common violet snail (E Australia).
(i) *Bellastraea sirius*—common tent shell (Long Reef, NSW).
(j) *Subninella undulata*—warrener or lightning turban (Port Noarlunga, SA).
(k) *Tylospira scutulata*—ostrich foot shell (off Sydney).
(l) *Amoria (Amorena) undulata*—wavy volute (Two-fold Bay, NSW).
(m) *Vicimitra contermina*—black mitre (Long Reef).
(n) *Cronia pseudamygdala*—fake-almond purple (Minnie Waters, near Grafton, NSW).
(o) *Conuber melastoma*—red-mouthed sand snail (Gunnamatta Bay, near Sydney, NSW).
(p) *Dinassovica militaris*—military turban (Wooli).

Plate 38.

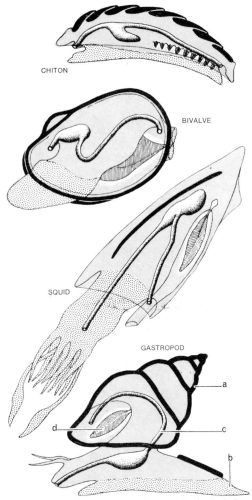

Fig. 47. The four main molluscan subgroups showing body form and structural relationships: *a*, shell indicated in heavy black; *b*, foot stippled; *c*, gut shaded; *d*, gills lined.

with a mantle, foot, head and radula. There are sometimes oral tentacles, and a pair of sensitive organs with eyes, the rhinophores, are usually present on the upper surface towards the anterior end (pl. 39 top). A tuft of plume-like gills may be situated on the upper surface behind the rhinophores. Many different nudibranchs, ranging in length up to 12 inches or more, have been recorded from Australia, but little is known of their detailed distribution and habits in this area.

The bivalved molluscs or pelecypods include many species of direct economic importance to man. Scallops, edible oysters, pearl oysters, clams and pipis all have a pair of shells and all belong to this major group. Representative bivalves range in size from the largest molluscs known, the giant *Tridacna* clams of northern Barrier Reef waters, with shells up to about 3 feet in length and 500 pounds in weight, down to tiny paired shells a fraction of an inch in length. The two valves, or shells, of the group are usually more or less symmetrical and of equal size. They are formed on the left and right sides of the animal and are fastened together on the upper edge by an elastic horny ligament. When relaxed, the shells are held open by this ligament, but can be closed by the contraction of two large muscles which usually leave attachment scars on the inside of each valve.

Examples of many different bivalve types from the southern half of Australia are shown in plate 40. Scallops and jingle shells are well known, while venus, tellen and cockle shells are also common. File shells and living-fossil trigonias, or brooch shells (pl. 40g), are characteristic of this area.

Key to opposite page:

Plate 39. Nudibranch molluscs; *Polycera capensis* on colonial ascidian *(top)*; *Madrella sanguinea (bottom left)*; *Armina cygnea (bottom right)*.

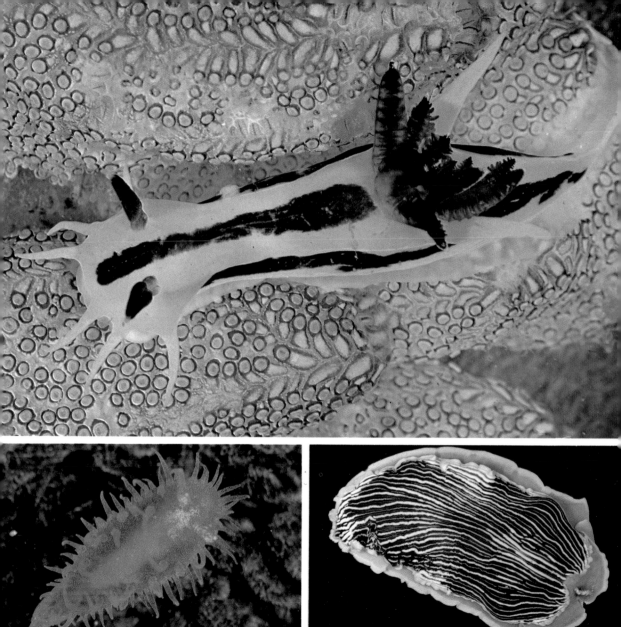

Squids, octopuses, cuttlefish and their allies are usually regarded as the most highly developed and specialised of all the molluscs, in fact the most highly developed of all the invertebrates. Their large, non-closing eyes, like those of vertebrates and quite unlike the eyes of any other invertebrate, their obvious intelligence, their proved memory and their ability to learn, all serve to set the cephalopods apart from all other non-vertebrate creatures.

In the Cephalopoda, or "head-footed" animals, the foot is divided into a number of "arms" encircling the head (fig. 47). As in the gastropods, all degrees of shell reduction are found in these animals. The pearly nautilus, for example, has a large, external, coiled shell while the ramshorn squid has a small, internal, coiled shell (pl. 37d); cuttlefish have a thickened, internal cuttle bone (pl. 37a) and squids a flexible, horn-like, internal pen; octopuses,

Fig. 48. Scaly scallop, *Scaeochlamys lividus*, partly open showing numerous eyes and tentacles.

Plate 40. Key to opposite page:
(a) *Anomia descripta*—jingle shell (Sydney, NSW).
(b) *Bassina sidneyense*—Sydney venus shell (Sydney).
(c) *Neosolen correctus*—fingernail shell (Sydney).
(d) *Tellinota roseola*—pink tellen (Twofold Bay, NSW).
(e) *Austromactra rufescens*—trough shell (Mooball Beach, near Brunswick Heads, NSW).
(f) *Hemicardium hemicardium*—half cockle (King Reef, Qld).
(g) *Neotrigonia margaritacea*—pearly brooch shell (Twofold Bay).
(h) *Veletuceta flammea*—flame dog cockle (Lakes Entrance, Vic).
(i) *Austrolima nimbifer*—file shell (Sydney).
(j) *Fulvia racketti*—southern cockle (Sydney).
(k) *Musculus cumingianus*—three-area mussel (Lord Howe Island).
(l) *Chlamys asperrima*—doughboy scallop (Hobart, Tas).
(m) *Plebidonax deltoides*—pipi or ugari (Minnie Waters, near Grafton, NSW).
(n) *Striacallista disrupta*—disrupted venus (Evans Head, NSW).

Plate 40.

however, have no shell at all. The so-called "shell" of the paper nautilus (fig. 49) is not equivalent to the above structures, being merely a detachable casing secreted by the female of this pelagic, octopus-like cephalopod to hold eggs and to cradle hatching young.

One of the prettiest and most striking of all Australian octopuses is the small, blue-ringed octopus, *Hapalochlaena maculosa* (pl. 41 and fig. 50), immediately recognisable by the brilliant blue marks on the arms and body. It is common under rock ledges and in tidal rock pools, sometimes hiding in empty shells, and has been recorded from eastern, south-eastern and southern Australia. Unfortunately the venom of this pretty little animal has proved fatal to man. Human fatalities and near fatalities follow a fairly standard pattern. The octopus is found intertidally and placed on the back of the hand or arm while being shown to bystanders or while being carried up the beach. The victim is generally unaware of any actual bite but a speck of blood or a skin puncture may be seen. Within minutes, weakness, dryness or tingling of the mouth, numbness about the face, difficulty in breathing, and vomiting may occur. In severe cases partial or complete paralysis takes place and death can follow. Venom from the salivary glands of this octopus affects both nerves and muscles, bringing about complete cessation of all voluntary muscle activity, hence death is due to respiratory failure and the heart is mainly unaffected. Recent studies by the Commonwealth Serum Laboratories suggest that the blue-ringed octopus is unique in the toxicity of its venom, certainly surpassing that of any known land animal. Treatment consists in effective, and if necessary prolonged, artificial respiration.

Fig. 49. Shell-like egg-case of paper nautilus, *Argonauta nodosa*, usually found beach-stranded.

Fig. 50. Small and venomous blue-ringed octopus, *Hapalochlaena*, from south-eastern rock pools.

Plate 41. The venomous blue-ringed octopus, *Hapalochlaena maculosa*.

LACEWORK WITH BEAKS
bryozoans

BRYOZOANS, OR "MOSS ANIMALS" as the name means, build up colonial growths of many different shapes and forms. These colonies are usually attached to algal fronds, rocks, or some other fixed object in the sea, but may be unattached and free-living on sand or mud bottoms. Bryozoan growths can be flexible, soft, and plant-like (referred to as sea-mosses) or hard, calcareous and regularly or irregularly branched (referred to as lace-corals, pl. 42). Some form flat, encrusting films over the surfaces on which they are growing (sea-mats), others form free-living, disc-like growths (fig. 52), while a few grow as irregular gelatinous masses.

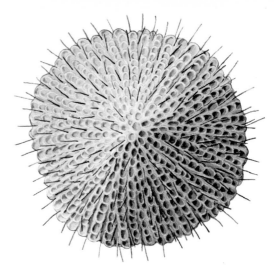

Fig. 52. Free-living, button-like colony of *Lunulites capulus* from offshore sand-bottoms.

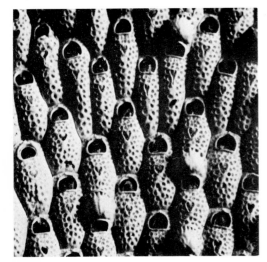

Fig. 51. Photomicrograph of colonial sea-mat, *Fenestrulina mutabilis*, showing individual empty cells.

The microscopically-sized, individual bryozoan lives in a protective, horny or calcareous cell, into which it can withdraw completely. The surface appearance of a colony depends to a great extent on the order and arrangement of these individual cells, or zooecia as they are called, and the position of the cell aperture (fig. 51). The zooid, or animal within the cell, consists mainly of a U-shaped alimentary canal with a ring or horseshoe of ciliated tentacles around the mouth, and a set of muscles for extending and retracting these tentacles. In some bryozoans, such as one of the common boat-fouling *Bugula* species, there are specially reduced and modified individuals called avicularia in addition to the normal feeding zooids. They resemble tiny birds' heads, complete with snapping beaks; their function appears to be preventing larvae or other small animals from settling on the colony and interfering with feeding activities.

Plate 42. Lace-bryozoan, *Sertella granulata,* and brittle star, *Opiothrix caespitosa.*

SPINES AND FIVE-FOLD SYMMETRY
echinoderms

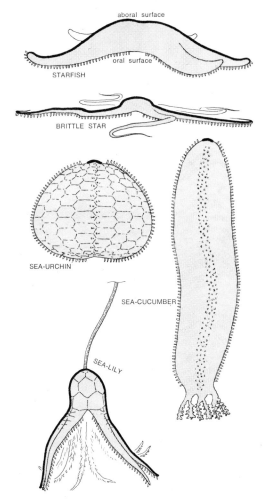

aboral surface

oral surface

STARFISH

BRITTLE STAR

SEA-URCHIN

SEA-CUCUMBER

SEA-LILY

T HE ECHINODERMS, or the "spiny-skinned" animals, have a body plan completely different from that of any other animal group. They are what is called radially symmetrical, that is, they can be divided into two similar pieces by a cut in any direction through the mouth and central axis of the body. Superimposed on this basic radial symmetry (which in fact is secondarily acquired as echinoderm larvae are bilaterally symmetrical) there is often a five-fold, or pentamerous symmetry. Thus organs, appendages, and other structures are serially repeated five times around the central axis of the body. The mysterious "rule of five" in body organisation occurs only in the echinoderms and in one other obscure and unrelated group of burrowing worms. Coupled with the placement of the mouth at the centre of the lower surface in most forms, this five-fold plan is unique to the echinoderms in the animal kingdom.

Living, as distinct from fossil, echinoderms are divided, by coincidence, into five very clearly separated and easily distinguished subgroups (fig. 53). There are asteroids or starfish (alternative name: sea-stars; pl. 43), which show a great variety of size and form. These have five or more hollow arms with parts of the digestive system enclosed, though in extreme cases the arms are so short they are not readily distinguishable from the body and the animal is more or less pentagonal or hexagonal. There are ophiuroids or brittle stars (alternative names: serpent stars, snake stars; fig. 58) with five solid, slender and more or less extensively segmented arms, which in some specialised members are arborescent or multi-branched (the basket stars,

Fig. 53. The five main echinoderm subgroups showing body form and relative extent of oral, or mouth, surface (line with small projections) and aboral, or opposite to mouth, surface (solid black line). Examples are drawn in the same relative position.

Plate 43. The blue linckia, *Linckia laevigata*, on coral rubble.

Fig. 54. The temperate sea-urchin, *Centrostephanus rodgersii.*

pl. 46). Then there are echinoids or sea-urchins (alternative names: sea-eggs, sand dollars, heart urchins; fig. 54 and pl. 45), which are encased in a firm, usually rigid test, more or less covered with spines, and with no projecting arms. The test is commonly rounded, with the lower or oral surface somewhat flattened, but the shape can range from ellipsoidal to discoidal. The spines can be hollow or solid, and range in size from virtually microscopic, through extremely long and slender, as in the needle-spined urchin, *Diadema*, to thickened, heavy and blunt, as in the slate-pencil urchins.

The holothurians or sea-cucumbers (alternative names: bêche-de-mer, trepang; fig. 59) are unlike the other subgroups in that the characteristic echinoderm calcareous skeleton is reduced to minute scattered plates and the body wall is usually soft. The body is elongated and the animal lies on one side with the mouth at the anterior end. Finally the crinoids or sea-lilies (alternative name: feather stars; pl. 47) are at once recognisable by their many feather-like arms, and by the presence at the centre of their aboral surface (the surface opposite to that with the mouth) of either a cluster of slender and short appendages called cirri (free-living forms), or, in some rare species, a more or less elongated stalk (attached forms). In contrast to the other subgroups, crinoids normally live with the mouth, or oral surface, uppermost and the cirri or stalk in contact with the bottom.

Despite the very great differences in shape and appearance shown by the diverse members of these various subgroups, echinoderms in general share a number of anatomical and physiological features that set them aside from other animals. Thus in addition to five-fold symmetry, they possess an internal skeleton of calcareous plates, often supporting external spines; they possess numerous extensible and elastic tube feet powered by a seawater hydraulic system, and they show an

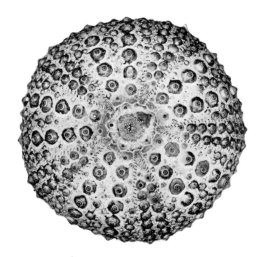

Fig. 55. Cleaned test of *Centrostephanus rodgersii.*

Plate 44. Sculptured spines of the sea-urchin, *Centrostephanus rodgersii.* ⇨

amazing faculty for the regeneration of lost or damaged parts of the body.

The relative rigidity of most echinoderms is provided by a meshwork skeleton embedded in the soft flesh. This is made up of plates or ossicles in numerous shapes and sizes, differing from species to species, but each unit formed by a single individual crystal of calcium carbonate. The flexibility of such a skeleton is due to the individual plates not being directly fused to one another. The sea-urchins, however, have the whole body enclosed in a more or less globular structure or test, as seen in the photograph of *Centrostephanus* (fig. 55). Here the individual plates fit together very closely, as in a mosaic, and show the regularly placed tubercles or bosses which support the numerous long spines in life. The five-fold symmetry of this test can be seen clearly in the arrangement of the circle of plates in the centre of the aboral surface and in the radiating zones of regularly-sized tubercles.

Some starfish have a soft fleshy surface through which the skeletal plates can only be felt, but most have a hard and more or less rough surface with an obvious skeletal structure. The individual plates can be large and regularly arranged as in *Pentagonaster dubeni* (frontispiece) or small, very numerous and lacking distinct regularity, as in *Linckia laevigata* (pl. 43). The reduced and scattered plates in the skin of a sea-cucumber can be seen in detail only with a microscope. They usually show remarkable regularity, and are often very complex, as in the six-spoke wheel plates of *Chiridota* (fig. 60).

The hydraulic-pressure, tube-feet system of echinoderms is used for locomotion and feeding in many species, though in some it is greatly reduced. In starfish, water enters this system through minute openings in the asymmetrically-placed sieve plate on the aboral surface (frontispiece, between the two lower arms) and is drawn by the beating of minute cilia down a tube into the ring canal, encircling the centre of the body. From this circular canal, five or more radial canals arise, one for each arm. These connect by short side branches with many pairs of hollow, thin-walled, highly extensible tube feet projecting in two rows from the under surface of each arm. Each tube foot has a rounded muscular sac at its base and an expanded sucker at its tip. When the sac contracts, water, prevented by a valve from flowing back into the radial canal, is forced under pressure into the tube foot. The elastic foot extends and attaches to the bottom by its sucker. The longitudinal muscles of the tube foot then contract, shortening it, forcing water back into the sac and drawing the animal forward. Hundreds of tube feet acting in concert move the starfish over a hard bottom, walk it over soft sand and mud, or even enable it to pull open a bivalve shellfish by

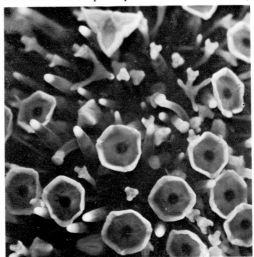

Fig. 56. Flower-like pedicellarial pincers of the sea-urchin *Toxopneustes pileolus.*

Plate 45. The venomous sea-urchin, *Toxopneustes pileolus.*

working in relays to tire the closing muscles of the shells. As the bivalve opens, the starfish extends part of its stomach through its mouth, envelops the soft parts of the shellfish and digests them.

Sea-urchin tube feet are typically arranged in five double rows radiating out from the centre of the aboral surface and then converging on to the mouth in the centre of the lower surface. Figure 55 shows the series of small pores in the test through which the tube feet project (each double row starting as a V from the circle of plates in the centre). The sieve plate of the hydraulic system is the dark triangular ossicle to the upper right of the central circle.

Brittle star tube feet are without suckers, but ophiuroids move mainly by snake-like movements of their arms and by the action of their arm spines, though not all species have arms or spines as

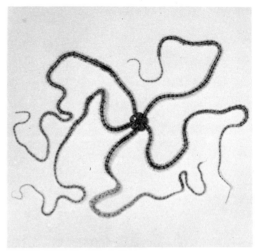

Fig. 58. The long-armed, tropical brittle star, *Macrophiothrix longipeda.*

Fig. 57. Mouth and under surface of body of brittle star, *Macrophiothrix longipeda.*

well-developed as those of *Macrophiothrix longipeda* (figs. 57 & 58). Holothurian tube feet are more strongly developed on the side on which the animal lies and moves, while crinoid tube feet are on the upper surface of the arms as might be expected in these functionally turned over animals. In the latter group, they are not used in locomotion, but assist in feeding and, as in all echinoderms, act as extra respiratory organs.

There are nearly 800 species of echinoderms known from Australian waters. They are found from intertidal rock pools down to the slopes beyond the continental shelf; they range in colour from dull greys and browns to brilliant reds, yellows, and blues, and range in size from less than half an inch across in some brittle stars to at least 6 feet in length in some holothurians.

Plate 46. The basket star, *Conocladus amblyconus.*

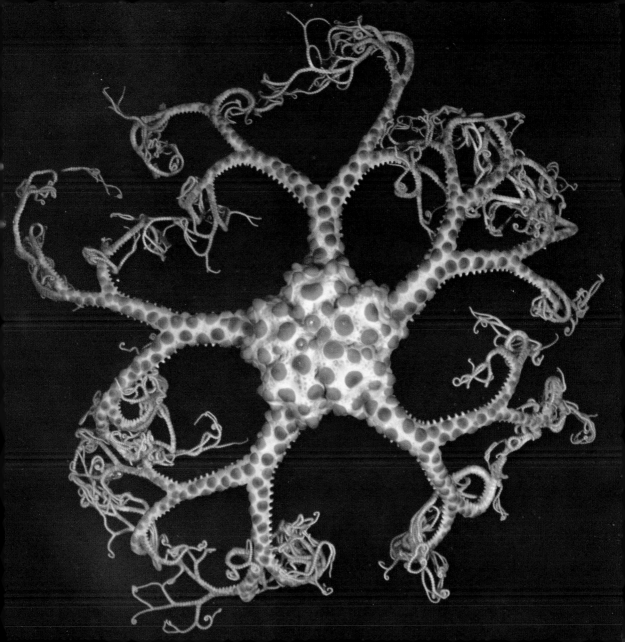

The long-armed *Macrophiothrix longipeda* (fig. 58) is a tropical ophiuroid common on the Barrier Reef, and provides a strong contrast to the bizarre basket star, *Conocladus amblyconus* (pl. 46), from New South Wales. The latter is a commensal species found at depths of about 60 feet or more, entwined in various alcyonarian fan corals and firm hydroid growths. The holothurian, *Chiridota gigas* (fig. 59), is known from south-eastern Australia, but a related species, with very similar wheel plates, occurs in tropical waters. The delicately-coloured comasterid feather star shown in plate 47 is in a typical feeding position, with its numerous arms constantly on the move. Feather stars in general are not well-known in Australian waters and many brightly-coloured and distinctly-patterned species cannot be named with certainty as yet.

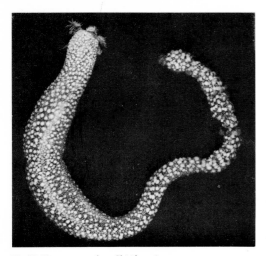

Fig. 59. The sea-cucumber, *Chiridota gigas.*

The vermilion biscuit star, *Pentagonaster dubeni* (frontispiece), is found in south-eastern and southern Australia from low tide level to a depth of at least 100 feet. Its brilliant colour brings it readily to the attention of skindivers and underwater photographers. The incredibly vivid *Linckia laevigata* (pl. 43), is locally abundant in many areas of the Barrier Reef and is often seen lying fully exposed in open pools or on patches of coral rubble. *Centrostephanus rodgersii* is a large, shallow-water urchin, common in southern New South Wales, while the beautiful *Toxopneustes pileolus* (pl. 45) has only recently been recorded for the first time in Australia. Previously known from Japan and other areas in the Pacific, *Toxopneustes* is now known from Queensland and New South Wales. The flower-like pincers (fig. 56) are reputedly capable of giving a venomous "bite" and may have caused the death of several Japanese divers.

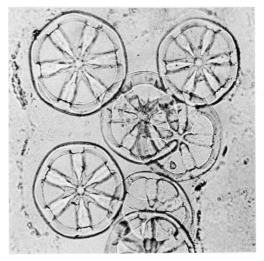

Fig. 60. Calcareous, wheel plates in skin of *Chiridota gigas* (approx. x325).

Plate 47. A comasterid feather star from Barrier Reef waters.

SEA-SQUIRTS AND TULIPS
tunicates

SOME OF THE advanced invertebrates have features, such as a flexible supporting rod in their larvae (foreshadowing a backbone) and slits in the pharynx wall (like a shark's gills), approaching those typical of verbetrate animals. These are the tunicates, named from their tough, protective "tunic" or outer body layer. Included here are the attached ascidians ranging from solitary sea-squirts (for example cunjevoi, pl. 4) and stalked sea-tulips (pl. 48) to colonial and encrusting forms, such as the yellow individuals seen in the background to plate 39, as well as the planktonic salps and pyrosomas. The salps are mainly small and solitary but the latter form elongate, hollow, cigar-shaped colonies which may, at times, reach enormous size (fig. 61).

Fig. 61. Giant colony of free-floating *Pyrosoma spinosum*, seen off southern NSW. Drawing based on underwater photographs.

Plate 48. The sea-tulip, *Pyura pachydermatina.*

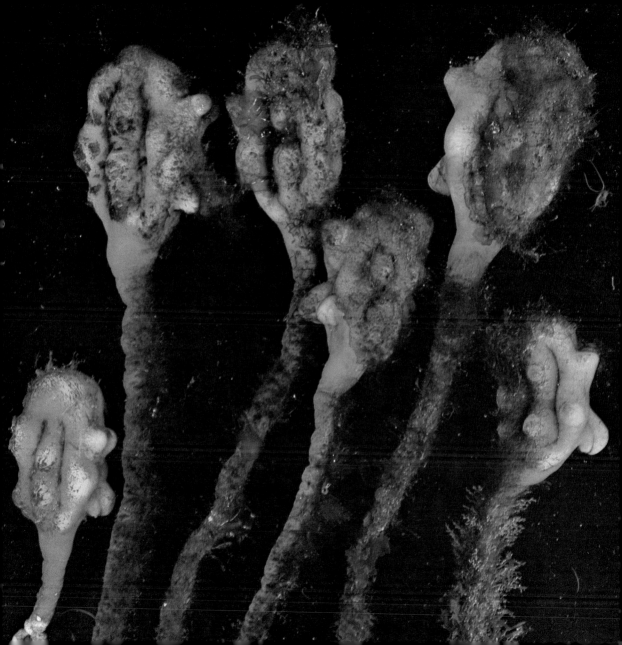

BACKBONES AND FINS
fish

THERE ARE ABOUT 2,300 species of marine fish now known from the Australian area. This number will certainly be increased when more is known of the fauna from offshore deep waters. Fish may be defined as cold-blooded, aquatic, vertebrate animals (that is possessing a vertebral column or backbone), breathing with gills and moving through the water by means of fins. There are other vertebrates in the sea, such as sea-snakes, turtles, dolphins, and whales, some quite fish-like in appearance, but none covered by the above definition.

No attempt can be made here to give even an outline of the variety of fish known from this area. Sharks and rays; eels, flying fish and flounders; mullet, parrot fish, and leatherjackets are only some of the groups represented in our diverse fauna. Plate 49 shows the striking and distinctive old wife, a common shallow water species from rocky areas of south-eastern and southern Australia. Figures 62

and 63 contrast a mangrove swamp mudskipper, which spends considerable periods out of the water, with one of the little, deepwater, lure-bearing monsters which are occasionally stranded on our seashores.

Fig. 63. Black, scaleless *Idiacanthus niger*, sometimes stranded as deepwater "mini-monster"

Fig. 62. Large-scaled mudskipper, *Periophthalmodon australis*, on tropical mangrove branch.

Plate 49. Old wife, *Enoplosus armatus*.

COLD-BLOODED AIR BREATHERS
turtles and sea-snakes

THERE ARE FIVE species of marine turtles in Australian waters. Three, the green turtle, the loggerhead, and the flatback turtle, breed on mainland beaches or offshore islands in the area, while two, the hawksbill turtle and the luth, though common as visitors, do not breed in this country. The flatback, or pygmy green, is uncommon and known only from Northern Territory coastal waters, but the loggerhead and the green are both common in tropical Australia and are seen occasionally off southern temperate Australia.

Green turtles reach a length of about 4 feet and can weigh as much as 300 pounds; they are now totally protected by special legislation throughout Queensland. From the end of October until early in May, females come ashore at night to lay eggs on various islands in the Barrier Reef area. After burying between 50 and 200 eggs in a nest, they

Fig. 65. Hatchling green turtle, *Chelonia mydas*, Heron Island, Capricorn Group.

move back to the sea again, leaving a return track with a central tail drag (pl. 50) quite different from their track up the beach. The eggs take six to ten weeks to hatch. The hatchlings (fig. 65) then work their way up through the sand and immediately make their way to the sea, running a gauntlet of silver gulls by day or ghost crabs by night.

About twenty species of sea-snakes are found in Australia. All have nostrils on the top of the head (fig. 64), which are sealed by valve flaps when the animal is under water. All have the tail flattened from side to side and paddle-shaped, and, with a few exceptions, all bear their young alive at sea. All are venomous and all must be treated as potentially dangerous, though generally speaking sea-snakes are curious rather than aggressive.

Fig. 64. Head of sea-snake, *Astrotia stokesii*, from tropical reef waters.

Plate 50. Female green turtle, *Chelonia mydas*, returning to the sea.

HAIR AND WARM BLOOD
marine mammals

CONTRASTED WITH THE cold-blooded reptiles of the preceding section, the marine mammals (whales, dolphins, seals, and the dugong, or sea cow) are warm-blooded and insulated with a layer of blubber and, in the case of the seals, hair. The whales and dolphins, or cetaceans as they are called, are virtually hairless and superficially fish-like in general appearance. Their streamlined bodies have a prominent dorsal fin, lack hind limbs and have a tail modified into two horizontal flukes. Nevertheless they are true mammals, bearing their young alive and suckling them on milk.

Fig. 66. Bottle-nosed dolphin, *Tursiops truncatus*, taking fish.

Many cetaceans occur in the Australian area and several of the larger whales, such as the humpback and the right whale, used to come and occasionally still come into shallow coastal waters to breed. Three species, the sperm whale, the humpback and the right, have been hunted extensively by man in this area and the last is now a rare animal throughout its entire range. Dolphins of several types, including the bottle-nosed dolphin, *Tursiops truncatus* (fig. 66), and Risso's dolphin, occur in coastal waters and display the characteristic behaviour of many small cetaceans—swimming alongside and crossing the bows of moving ships.

Three different seals (two fur seals and the Australian sea-lion, or hair seal) live and breed along the southern Australian coastline. Early last century the southern elephant seal occupied large breeding colonies in the Tasmanian area, but it was soon exterminated there by hunters and now breeds no nearer than Macquarie Island in the subantarctic.

The Australian fur seal, *Arctocephalus doriferus*, ranges from New South Wales to Victoria and Tasmania, breeding in scattered colonies on certain offshore islands and isolated coastal areas. Adult males reach a length of about 7 feet. The smaller New Zealand fur seal, *Arctocephalus forsteri*, though concentrated mainly in the New Zealand area, also breeds on several small islands off the coasts of South Australia and southern Western Australia. The Australian sea-lion, *Neophoca cinerea* (pl. 51), is a large animal; adult males may grow to a length of about 10 feet. It is easily recognisable by the patch of white hair on the crown and nape of the neck in adult males. Females are considerably smaller and the throat and belly are dirty white in colour. Sea-lions live in groups on various offshore islands between Adelaide in South Australia and the Abrolhos in Western Australia.

Plate 51. Male Australian sea-lion, *Neophoca cinerea.*

FEATHERS AND FLIGHT
sea birds

SEA BIRDS are such an integral part of the seashore scene that they must be considered here, even though they nest on land, often away from beaches, and may spend much of their time in the air. By sea birds we mean those birds which are truly dependent on the sea or the seashore for their existence. Therefore both oceanic birds such as petrels and gannets, and shore birds such as penguins, shags, herons, waders, gulls, and terns are included within the meaning of this term.

The little, or fairy, penguin (*Eudyptula minor*) is the only penguin breeding in the Australian area. It ranges around our eastern and southern coasts and offshore islands from southern Queensland to north of Perth. When ashore it is nocturnal and seldom seen by day. Another nocturnal bird, at least when ashore in the breeding season, is the wedge-tailed shearwater, *Puffinus pacificus* (fig. 67). This northern muttonbird breeds on many scattered islands in the Barrier Reef area and off Western Australia, from the vicinity of Perth north to about Port Hedland. Like most of the other smaller petrels it nests in burrows excavated in the sand or soil of the nesting colony. It does not migrate to the Northern Hemisphere in the non-breeding season as does the closely related, short-tailed shearwater, *Puffinus tenuirostris*, the "Tasmanian muttonbird" of commerce. This southern muttonbird breeds on islands off south-eastern Australia from southern New South Wales to eastern South Australia. Its annual migration takes it in a giant figure-of-eight across the Tasman Sea, through the northern New Zealand area, up and across the western Pacific and through Japanese waters to the Kurile and Aleutian Islands in the North Pacific, then down the Pacific coast of North America, back across the central Pacific and down the coast of eastern Australia to its nesting islands in Bass Strait and nearby waters.

There are at least nine different herons and egrets in Australia, but not all could be referred to as sea birds. The reef heron, *Egretta sacra*, however, is a true shore species and is found all around Australia, although it is commoner in tropical waters. It exists in two interbreeding colour phases, dark slate-grey and pure white, the white phase being more frequent in the north. The majority of the herons on Heron Island, Queensland, for example are white-phase birds.

The silver gull, *Larus novaehollandiae* (pl. 52), is the common gull throughout the Australian area. This beautiful red-billed bird is a typical beach scavenger and is one of the most strikingly coloured of all Australian seashore animals.

Fig. 67. Wedge-tailed shearwater or muttonbird, *Puffinus pacificus*, in nesting burrow, Heron Island.

Plate 52. The common silver gull, *Larus novaehollandiae*.

PHOTOGRAPHIC LOCATION LIST (Plates).

Frontispiece. Boat Harbour, Botany Bay, NSW, depth 45 ft.

Title page. Hat Head, near Kempsey, NSW.

Plate 1 (page 5). Soldier crabs, *Mictyris longicarpus*, Careel Bay, Pittwater, NSW.

Plate 2 (page 7). Stanwell Park, NSW, looking south. *Photo N. Marshall.*

Plate 3. Bermagui, NSW.

Plate 4. Long Reef, Collaroy, near Sydney, NSW.

Plate 5. Heron Island, Capricorn Group, Qld.

Plate 7. Palm Beach, NSW, from 1,500 ft. *Photo N. Marshall.*

Plates 8 & 9. Careel Bay, Pittwater, NSW.

Plate 10. Long Reef, Collaroy, NSW.

Plate 11. *(Top left and bottom right):* Bermagui, NSW. *(Top right):* Long Reef, NSW. *(Bottom left):* Port Kembla, NSW.

Plate 12. *(Left):* From 1,100 ft., off Heron Island, Qld. *Photo Miss A. Marshall.*

Plate 13. Heron Island, Qld.

Plate 14. Tamarama, Sydney, NSW.

Plate 15. Bronte Beach, Sydney, NSW.

Plate 16. Phase-contrast photomicrograph, Sydney, NSW.

Plate 17. Bronte Beach, Sydney, NSW.

Plate 18. Norah Head, NSW. *Photo F. G. Myers.*

Plate 19. Berowra Creek, Hawkesbury River, NSW. *Photo Howard Hughes, Australian Museum.*

Plate 20. Bare Island, La Perouse, NSW, depth 30 ft.

Plate 21. Tamarama, Sydney, NSW.

Plate 22. Off Cronulla, NSW, depth 60 ft.

Plate 23. Bare Island, NSW, depth 40 ft.

Plate 24. Bare Island, NSW, depth 45 ft.

Plate 25. Off Manly, Port Jackson, depth 20 ft.

Plate 26. Hat Head, near Kempsey, NSW.

Plates 27 & 28. Long Reef, Collaroy, NSW.

Plate 29. Careel Bay, Pittwater, NSW.

Plate 30. Long Reef, Collaroy, NSW.

Plate 31. Bronte Beach, Sydney, NSW.

Plate 32. George's River, near Sydney, NSW.

Plate 33. "Ship Rock", Burraneer Bay, Port Hacking, NSW, depth 15 ft.

Plate 34. "Ship Rock", Port Hacking, NSW, depth 55 ft. *Photo Walter Deas.*

Plate 35. Burraneer Bay, Port Hacking, NSW.

Plate 36. Minnie Waters, near Grafton, NSW, April, 1964. *Photo Anthony Healy.*

Plate 39. *(Top):* "Ship Rock", Port Hacking, NSW, depth 25 ft. *(Bottom left):* Minnie Waters, NSW. *(Bottom right):* Botany Bay, NSW, depth 20 ft. *Photos Anthony Healy.*

Plate 41. Camp Cove, Port Jackson, NSW, depth 15 ft.

Plate 42. "Ship Rock", Port Hacking, NSW, depth 35 ft.

Plate 43. Heron Island, Qld.

Plate 44. Camp Cove, Port Jackson, NSW.

Plate 45. Camp Cove, Port Jackson, NSW, depth 10 ft.

Plate 46. Bare Island, La Perouse, Sydney, NSW, depth 50 ft.

Plate 47. Heron Island, Qld. *Photo H. G. Cogger.*

Plate 48. Fairlight, Port Jackson, Sydney, NSW.

Plate 49. "Ship Rock", Port Hacking, NSW, depth 50 ft. *Photo Walter Deas.*

Plate 50. Heron Island, Qld, after egg-laying, December.

Plate 51. Seal Beach, Kangaroo Island, SA. *Photo B. J. Marlow.*

Plate 52. South West Rocks, Trial Bay, NSW.

Jacket front. South West Rocks, Trial Bay, and Laggers Point.

Jacket back. Stinging anemone, *Anthothoe* sp., offshore reefs, NSW.

PHOTOGRAPHIC LOCATION LIST (Figs.).

Fig. 3. Tamarama, Sydney, NSW.

Fig. 8. Seven Mile Beach, Gerroa, NSW. *Photo Elizabeth Pope.*

Figs. 10 & 11. Careel Bay, Pittwater, NSW.

Fig. 12. Tamarama, Sydney, NSW.

Figs. 13 & 14. Off Otago, NZ. *Electron micrographs W. S. Bertaud, DSIR, NZ.*

Fig. 15. Off Heron Island, Capricorn Group, Qld.

Fig. 17. Tamarama, Sydney, NSW.

Fig. 19. Bronte Beach, Sydney, NSW.

Fig. 21. Lavender Bay, Port Jackson, NSW.

Fig. 24. Coogee Beach, Sydney, NSW.

Fig. 25. Off Cronulla, NSW, depth 60 ft.

Fig. 26. Bare Island, La Perouse, NSW, depth 40 ft.

Fig. 28. Bare Island, NSW, depth 45 ft.

Fig. 29. Off Manly, Port Jackson, depth 20 ft.

Figs. 30 & 31. Hat Head, near Kempsey, NSW.

Fig. 32. Long Reef, Collaroy, near Sydney, NSW.

Figs. 33 & 34. Heron Island, Qld.

Fig. 35. Long Reef, Collaroy, NSW.

Fig. 37. Heron Island, Qld. *Photo Anthony Healy.*

Fig. 38. Tamarama, Sydney, NSW.

Fig. 40. Church Point, Pittwater, NSW.

Fig. 41. Heron Island, Qld.

Fig. 42. Port Jackson, Sydney, NSW.

Fig. 43. Ned's Beach, Lord Howe Island.

Fig. 44. Careel Bay, Pittwater, NSW.

Fig. 45. Tamarama, Sydney, NSW.

Fig. 46. Long Reef, Collaroy, NSW.

Fig. 48. Bare Island, NSW, depth 20 ft.

Fig. 49. Wollongong, NSW.

Fig. 50. Camp Cove, Port Jackson, NSW, depth 15 ft.

Fig. 51. *Photo G. C. Clutton, Australian Museum.*

Fig. 52. Off Norah Head, NSW, depth 26-38 fms. *Records Australian Museum Vol. 13, p. 191.*

Figs. 54 & 55. Port Jackson, Sydney, NSW.

Fig. 56. Camp Cove, Port Jackson, NSW, depth 10 ft.

Figs. 57 & 58. Heron Island, Qld.

Figs. 59 & 60. Long Reef, Collaroy, NSW.

Fig. 61. Near Nowra, NSW. *Based on underwater photos by Norm Leibick.*

Fig. 62. Cairns, Qld. *Photo H. V. Chargois.*

Fig. 63. Cook Strait, NZ. *Photo M. D. King, Victoria University, NZ.*

Figs. 64 & 65. Heron Island, Qld.

Fig. 66. Taronga Zoological Park, Sydney, NSW.

Fig. 67. Heron Island, Qld.

INDEX
Bold figures indicate colour plates or black and white figures